THE PALEO INSTANT POT COOKBOOK FOR BEGINNERS

THE PALEO INSTANT POT COOKBOOK FOR BEGINNERS

PRESSURE COOKER RECIPES MADE CLEAN

Kinsey Jackson, MS, CNS, CFMP

Sally Johnson, MA, RD, LD, CFMP

Photography by Darren Muir

ROCKRIDGE
PRESS

For general information on our other products and services or to obtain technical support, please contact our Customer Care Department within the United States at (866) 744-2665, or outside the United States at (510) 253-0500.

Rockridge Press publishes its books in a variety of electronic and print formats. Some content that appears in print may not be available in electronic books, and vice versa.

TRADEMARKS: Rockridge Press and the Rockridge Press logo are trademarks or registered trademarks of Callisto Media Inc. and/or its affiliates, in the United States and other countries, and may not be used without written permission. All other trademarks are the property of their respective owners. Rockridge Press is not associated with any product or vendor mentioned in this book.

Cover image: Roast Beef and Roots, page 78.
Interior and Cover Designer: Erin Yeung
Art Producer: Samantha Ulban
Editor: Van Van Cleave
Production Editor: Rachel Taenzler
Production Manager: Michael Kay

Photography © 2021 Darren Muir. Food styling by Yolanda Muir. Kinsey Jackson's author photo courtesy of Naomi D. Sheikin Photography. Sally Johnson's author photo courtesy of Mark Hiebert of Hiebert Photography.

Instant Pot is a registered trademark of Instant Brands Inc. Callisto Media and its products and services are not endorsed by, sponsored by, or affiliated with Instant Brands Inc. Our use of the Instant Pot trademark and any related names, logos, and brands is for identification purposes only, and does not imply any such endorsement, sponsorship, or affiliation.

ISBN: Print 978-1-64876-997-9
eBook 978-1-64876-998-6

R0

This book is dedicated to those who want to feel better and do better, in less time, with less effort.

Contents

Introduction viii

Chapter 1: Getting Started with Paleo 1

Chapter 2: Getting to Know Your Instant Pot 15

Chapter 3: Breakfast 27

Chapter 4: Soups and Stews 37

Chapter 5: Poultry Mains 49

Chapter 6: Seafood Mains 65

Chapter 7: Beef Mains 77

Chapter 8: Pork Mains 91

Chapter 9: Vegetarian Mains and Sides 103

Instant Pot Timing Charts 119

Measurement Conversions 122

Resources 123

References 124

Index 127

Introduction

Welcome to *The Paleo Instant Pot Cookbook for Beginners*! This book is your guide to enjoying delicious and healing Paleo foods at the touch of a button with your Instant Pot. Are you new to the Paleo diet? Do you have an Instant Pot still sitting in its box, unopened? Whether you're a total newbie or a seasoned pro, this book will have you dining on mouthwatering Paleo Instant Pot meals in no time at all.

For as long as humans have roamed this earth, we have been eating a Paleo diet. It is only very recently that grains, beans, dairy, and liquid oils have become a part of our regular diets. Rather, we've survived and thrived off meats, vegetables, fruits, nuts, seeds, and eggs. This is the diet that has nourished humans for the vast majority of the time we have been here on Earth; it's no wonder that these are the very foods that optimize our health.

While giving up grains, sugar, and dairy may sound impossible, we assure you that it's not hard. In fact, it's probably a lot easier than what you've been doing previously. You'll quickly realize that eating Paleo is far from another boring, bland, restrictive diet. Having more energy and feeling your best will help keep you motivated as well!

As Paleo nutritionists, we've helped thousands of individuals across the globe transform their health, and on a personal level, we've both experienced how life-changing eating Paleo can be. After following a vegetarian diet for nearly 25 years, Kinsey was diagnosed with multiple autoimmune diseases, including rheumatoid arthritis, lupus, hypothyroidism, and alopecia. By transitioning from vegetarian to Paleo, she used food as her medicine to reverse her autoimmunity and keep it in remission. By rejecting the standard dietary advice and adopting a Paleo diet and lifestyle, Sally lost unwanted pounds that had been creeping up over the years and resolved two decades of irritable bowel syndrome (IBS), gastroesophageal reflux disease (GERD), periodontitis, and other debilitating inflammatory conditions. We know firsthand the power of Paleo, and we can't wait for you to experience it too!

But those incredible results came at a price. We spent hours in the kitchen, day after day, which was exhausting and threatened our ability to stay the Paleo course. As working full-time moms, we didn't have the time or energy to spend all day cooking. When the Instant Pot made its debut in 2010, we hopped on board and are so glad we did! The Instant Pot drastically cut down our cooking time and made it so much easier to stick to Paleo. Combining modern tools such as the Instant Pot with an ancestral way of eating is truly a winning combination for lifelong health.

We're so excited for you to discover how it feels to fuel your body with the foods that nature intended, and to be empowered by cooking meats, veggies, and so much more in your Instant Pot. Chapter 1 of this book will introduce you to the Paleo diet: what it is, why it works, and everything you need to know. Chapter 2 will give you the confidence you need to use the Instant Pot for almost any meal. The remainder of the book includes 75 delicious Paleo Instant Pot recipes that are easy to prepare and extremely satisfying.

Are you ready to jump-start your weight loss and achieve optimal health? You'll be there faster than you can imagine! We can't wait to take this journey with you, one delicious bite at a time.

In good health,

Kinsey Jackson, MS, CNS, CFMP

Sally Johnson, MA, RD, LD, CFMP

Sesame Bok Choy, page 114

CHAPTER 1

Getting Started with Paleo

Hello, friend, and welcome to the Paleo diet! This book will give you a quick, deep dive into the Paleo lifestyle and the Instant Pot. By the end of this chapter, you will understand the basic science behind why and how the Paleo diet works. You'll know which foods to eat and avoid, how to prep your kitchen, and answers to the most common FAQs when getting started. Whether or not you're new to Paleo, this book is going to help you reach your health goals faster than you ever thought possible!

What Is the Paleo Diet?

The Paleolithic (Paleo) diet is the original diet of humankind, meaning it is the way that humans have eaten as long as we have roamed this earth. It wasn't until the Agricultural Revolution, 10,000 years ago, that humans introduced grains, legumes, and dairy as main staples into their diet. While 10,000 years sounds like a long time, in the grand perspective of 2.5 million years of human evolution, it's a mere fraction of time (less than 0.5 percent) that we have been eating these modern foods.

The modern Paleo diet emphasizes foods that mimic our pre-Agricultural and pre-Industrial past, namely meat, vegetables, fruits, eggs, nuts, and seeds. Grains, beans, dairy, vegetable oils, sugar, and artificial foods are disallowed. We avoid these foods because the human body is not designed to process them. Obesity, chronic disease, and a laundry list of health problems represent an evolutionary mismatch between our current diet and what we are genetically programmed to eat. Although it is now the 21st century, there have been no significant human genome changes in the past 10,000 years. Physiologically speaking, we are still cave people!

Most diseases of modern civilization share a common root: chronic (long-term) inflammation, often stemming from an unhealthy gut. By returning to a traditional way of eating, you can heal your gut, banish inflammation, and start living the life you were intended to live: disease-free and vibrant!

The Science Behind the Paleo Diet

All it takes is a quick Google search to realize that people feel great eating Paleo. On top of the mountains of anecdotal evidence, researchers are beginning to prove what people are saying. As reported in the *American Journal of Clinical Nutrition*, people on the Paleo diet experienced greater reductions in waist circumference, triglyceride levels, blood pressure, and fasting blood glucose levels compared to diets following national nutrition guidelines.

Eating Paleo has these profound effects on health for two reasons. First, we are removing gut irritants, such as anti-nutrients found in grains and legumes, which in turn reduces inflammation. Second, the shift away from carbohydrates and toward healthy fats regulates blood sugar levels and supports a healthy microbiome. To date, hundreds of studies have demonstrated that a diverse gut microbiome is critical for many aspects of overall health. A 2019 cross-sectional study found an "unexpectedly high degree of biodiversity" in Paleo dieters' microbiomes, which closely resembles that of traditional hunter-gatherers.

Health Benefits

Paleo is an easy and effective way to reset your metabolism and achieve your optimal health, simply by eating the foods that Mother Nature intended. The benefits are truly too numerous to count and keep getting better the longer you live and eat this way! If you're a newbie, here are five reasons to get going on Paleo today.

To lose weight: Compared to typical diets, Paleo contains fewer carbohydrates and more healthy fats. The reduction of carbs and inflammatory foods results in rapid and long-lasting weight loss.

To reverse chronic disease: Eating an anti-inflammatory Paleo diet is the first essential step to reversing diseases and conditions of modern civilization like heart disease, diabetes, osteoporosis, cancer, dental issues, and autoimmune disorders, to name a few, which all share the common root of inflammation. Eating Paleo may also decrease your risk of developing these conditions in the first place.

For mood and mental clarity: People report the elimination of brain fog, improved energy, better memory, and a happier, more optimistic outlook on life!

To look and feel your best: When you banish inflammation, your skin clears up, you lean out, you feel lighter, your aches and pains disappear, and it's easier to move in your body.

To enhance athletic performance: After an initial buy-in period, athletic performance and recovery time can improve significantly.

Nutritional Breakdown: What to Eat

First and foremost, the Paleo diet starts with whole foods in their natural or minimally processed form. These foods provide your body with readily available fiber, nutrients, proteins, and healthy fats. For any given Paleo meal, at least half of your plate will be filled with vegetables and the other half with animal foods. About 20 percent of your calories will come from carbohydrates, 25 percent from proteins, and 55 percent from fats. In the following sections, we will break down the specific foods that make up these percentages.

Regarding alcohol and coffee, while they are technically Paleo, people will often benefit from removing these from their diet, at least for a while. Both can be hidden sources of sugar. If you drink coffee, avoid sweeteners and use a dairy-free creamer. For alcohol, avoid beer and grain-derived liquors, which are not Paleo, and opt for clear liquors over darker ones which contain more sugar. Dry wines, tequila, and vodka made from Paleo-friendly sources like potatoes and grapes are considered Paleo, in moderation.

ANIMAL PROTEIN

The Paleo diet emphasizes meat and seafood as the primary proteins; this is not a vegetarian-friendly diet. A pescatarian Paleo diet would be more feasible, but we encourage you to include as many types of meat as possible. Be courageous and try all the following varieties!

Red meat: All types, ideally grass-fed and grass-finished or pasture-raised, such as beef, pork, lamb, mutton, venison, goat, bison, or elk.

Poultry: All types, ideally pasture-raised, such as chicken, turkey, duck, or goose.

Seafood: All types of fish and seafood, ideally wild-caught. Opt for species known to be lower in mercury, such as salmon, herring, cod, sardines, anchovies, shrimp, clams, mussels, or oysters.

Organ meats: All types, ideally grass-fed or pasture-raised, such as liver, kidney, and heart, which are chock-full of vitamins and minerals that are hard to get elsewhere in a diet.

Some processed meats: Bacon, deli meats, sausage, and other processed meats are allowed if they do not contain chemical preservatives or additives and come from animals raised under healthy conditions.

FATS

Fats are a mainstay of the Paleo diet and will comprise more than half of your calories. Unfortunately, saturated fat and cholesterol have received undeserving bad reputations. Contrary to popular belief, neither are responsible for heart disease and may, in fact, help prevent it. Both the PURE study (2017), which followed more than 135,000 participants over a decade, and a state-of-the-art review by the *Journal of the American College of Cardiology* concluded that government limitations on and societal villainizing of saturated fats are not justified by science.

To this end, Paleo dieters do not fear saturated fats or cholesterol. Instead, we aim to limit our consumption of unhealthy polyunsaturated fats (PUFAs), such as canola, corn, soy, sunflower, safflower, and peanut oils, which contain high levels of inflammatory omega-6 fatty acids and are prone to releasing dangerous free radicals. In contrast, healthy PUFAs, such as extra-virgin olive oil, avocado oil, nut oils, and omega-3 fatty acids found in seafood and fish oil are encouraged. Be sure to store these oils in dark, airtight containers or the refrigerator to reduce oxidation. Healthy sources of saturated fats include coconut oil, ghee, grass-fed butter (if tolerated), and all types of animal fats (lard, tallow, bacon grease, schmaltz, duck fat, suet, etc.).

WHEAT AND OTHER GRAINS

A central premise of the Paleo diet is the exclusion of all types of grains, including wheat, rice, corn, quinoa, oats, and cereals. Grains and legumes contain chemicals called anti-nutrients that are irritating to the gut lining and trigger inflammation through a process known as "leaky gut." The gluten found in wheat is particularly destructive to the gut wall, though gluten-free grains can be just as damaging.

VEGETABLES

All types of vegetables are allowed on the Paleo diet, including dark leafy greens, sea vegetables, and root vegetables.

There is, however, some controversy surrounding whether or not potatoes should be considered Paleo. Due to their high carbohydrate content, it is easy to overconsume potatoes and other root vegetables, which are naturally higher in carbs. If you need to lower your blood sugars or have a lot of weight to lose, it is probably best to minimize all root vegetables. Otherwise, potatoes can be eaten in moderation.

Also controversial are peas and other green legumes, like snap peas and green beans. Although technically legumes, in their green state, they contain far fewer gut-irritating anti-nutrients than dried legumes and are well tolerated by most people. Feel free to use green beans, snap and snow peas, and other green legumes in moderation.

BEANS AND LEGUMES

Like grains, beans and legumes also contain anti-nutrients such as phytates and lectins and are therefore disallowed. In addition to irritating the gut, anti-nutrients interfere with the absorption of essential vitamins and minerals, so you do not adequately absorb them from your foods.

FRUITS

Fruit is allowed on the Paleo diet in moderation. We recommend keeping your consumption to two or fewer pieces per day, and always combined with fat and/or protein. While fruits offer an array of nutrients and antioxidants, they also contain a lot of natural sugars. Always consume fruit in its whole form, and avoid all types of fruit juice, a very concentrated sugar source. If you enjoy juicing, use a high-speed blender to blend the entire fruit and include twice as many vegetables as you do fruits. Rotate the types of fruit you eat; berries and melons are good options.

DAIRY

Dairy is also not permitted on the Paleo diet. Many people are unknowingly intolerant to dairy. When they remove it from their diet, they feel better and often experience a remission of various symptoms. Fret not: There are several Paleo-friendly alternatives. Full-fat coconut, nut, and seed milks can be used in place of regular milk. Nutritional yeast tastes a lot like cheese, and dairy-free yogurt made from nut or coconut milk is also allowed.

SUGARS

Sugar is one of the biggest roadblocks to weight loss and overall health. Most sugar sources are not Paleo, such as agave syrup, cane sugar/syrup, white and brown sugar, brown rice syrup, corn syrup, and anything ending in -ose. Artificial sweeteners such as Splenda, aspartame, Equal, and sucralose are also prohibited. Soda, sweetened beverages, and fruit juices fall under this category as well. Natural sweeteners like raw honey, maple syrup, molasses, monk fruit, stevia leaf, and coconut sugar can be consumed in moderation. Still, these sugar sources can interfere with weight loss and healing, so are best kept to a minimum.

SALT AND SPICES

All types of spices are allowed on the Paleo diet, ideally organic. Natural, unrefined salt (such as sea salt) is allowed. Like fat, salt has also received a bad reputation that it does not deserve. Sodium is essential for life and health. Processed salts like table salt should be avoided as they commonly contain preservatives, anti-caking agents, and other unhealthy chemicals.

You'll find that a moderate amount of sea salt is included in many recipes in this book. Feel free to increase or decrease the amount of salt in recipes to your liking and needs. In general, you can use salt liberally in your Paleo diet, as long as it is natural and unrefined.

PROCESSED FOODS

Though eating Paleo may sound intimidating or complicated, if you remember to eat whole, unrefined, unprocessed foods, you will be okay. When it comes to processed foods, we may think of unhealthy items like packaged donuts (definitely not Paleo!). In addition, many canned items are not Paleo; however, when not highly processed, they can be very useful for saving time in the kitchen (think: coconut milk, olives, or diced tomatoes). It is easy to cook fresh vegetables in the Instant Pot, but if needed, you can substitute canned or frozen in recipes; figure out what works for you!

To guide you in your journey, this quick-reference table summarizes which Paleo foods to enjoy freely, to have in moderation, and to avoid.

ENJOY	IN MODERATION	AVOID
All types of meat and eggs	High-quality deli meats, bacon, and other processed meats	Processed meats containing chemical additives
All types of wild seafood	Farmed seafood	Seafood containing high levels of mercury
All types of non-starchy vegetables	Starchy vegetables	Non-organic produce that appears on the EWG's Dirty Dozen list
Low-glycemic fruits such as avocado, limes, lemons	Most fruits	Fruit juices and other sugary drinks
Coconut products: cream and full-fat coconut milk	Grass-fed ghee and butter (if tolerated)	Dairy products
Healthy plant oils: coconut, avocado, olive	Nut and some seed oils: walnut, macadamia, sesame, flax, pumpkin	Unhealthy plant oils: vegetable, canola, sunflower, safflower, corn, soy, peanut
Pastured or organic animal fats: lard, tallow, schmaltz, and others	Conventional animal fats	Artificial *trans* fats
Organic herbs, spices, and natural unrefined salt	Conventional herbs and spices	Common table salt
Paleo-friendly foods in non-toxic packaging: coconut milk, tomatoes, olives, bone broth, protein bars, etc.	Minimally processed foods: nut butters, nut/seed/tuber flours, canned foods	Foods that are highly processed, refined, hydrogenated, or made from artificial ingredients
Water and herbal teas	Caffeine, coffee, and alcohol derived from non-grain sources	Coffee alternatives and alcohols derived from grains
	Green beans and peas	All beans and legumes
	Nuts and seeds and their butters, milks, and flours	All grains and their derivatives, peanuts and peanut butter
	Dark chocolate and natural sweeteners	Sugar and artificial sweeteners

Where and What to Buy

Buying Paleo foods doesn't have to break the bank, and you don't need to shop at specialty stores either. Most major grocery stores will have what you need, and other items can be found online. If possible, opt for organic vegetables and fruits, and avoid those listed on the Environmental Working Group's "Dirty Dozen" list. You'll discover that "in season" produce is much cheaper, and buying local is less expensive than imported items, which are also not as fresh. Talk to your local food co-ops and ranchers to find bulk discounts on meat. When possible, opt for meat that is hormone-free and raised without antibiotics.

Be Flexible and Develop an Attitude of Gratitude

Above all else, it's important not to feel deprived eating Paleo, or any diet for that matter. These days you can concoct a Paleo-friendly version of nearly any food. A quick Internet search will show you how easy it is to make Paleo breads, desserts, pasta, and more! Having said that, it can be a major loss to give up your familiar food favorites. Be kind with yourself as you venture down the Paleo path. If you fall off the wagon, don't beat yourself up. Use it as a learning opportunity: How does your body feel when you eat non-Paleo foods? Soon you'll start making associations between what you eat and how you feel, and once you do, it becomes much easier to stay the Paleo course.

Remember that the first few weeks of anything new are challenging. You may experience a detox phase as your body purges away old toxins that you've been carrying around for years. Headaches, bowel changes, fatigue, and irritability are all signs that your body is detoxing and a reassuring sign that you needed this change. Get plenty of rest and hydration to help speed the detox process along. Relaxing at mealtimes is one of the best things you can do for your overall health and digestion.

PALEO Q&A

1. **What if I have a food allergy, or I don't like a particular food?**

   You can swap out any meat, vegetable, or fruit with a similar food of the same quantity and adjust the recipe cooking times accordingly.

2. How will I get enough calcium without dairy?

It's easy to get enough calcium on the Paleo diet if you're mindful to eat your greens and bones (such as the soft ends of soup bones or small soft fish bones). Collard greens, canned salmon with bones, and turnip greens all provide more absorbable calcium than milk!

3. How do I eat Paleo at a restaurant?

Order dishes that contain only meat and non-starchy vegetables. Salads are a great option but ask for olive oil and vinegar as a dressing.

4. Do I need to take supplements?

In a perfect world, you would get all your nutrition from food. Due to the decreasing nutrient content of soils and impaired digestion, many people may not be meeting their nutritional needs across the board. Taking a high-quality, bioavailable multivitamin containing methylated or active nutrients is a good way to cover your bases. Other popular Paleo supplements include collagen powder, vitamin D, fish oil, and probiotics.

5. How does Paleo differ from Whole30?

Whole30 was modeled after Paleo and is designed as a 30-day challenge. It is stricter than Paleo, removing natural sweeteners and Paleo "treats." Many people do a strict 30-day Paleo challenge, then transition to an 80/20 diet, where they eat Paleo 80 percent of the time.

6. How does Paleo differ from the Keto diet?

The Keto diet is a very low-carbohydrate, high-fat (LCHF) diet that can lead to rapid weight loss and is used therapeutically for certain neurological disorders. We don't recommend it as a long-term diet unless medically indicated.

Your Instant Paleo Kitchen

Paleo is a return to healthy living, which starts in the kitchen. Let's walk through the basics of prepping your kitchen to make it Paleo. Take this opportunity to purge your pantry of all the unhealthy items that are holding you back from your goals!

Stock Up

Purchasing in bulk will save you money and trips to the store. The items listed here appear in several of the recipes in this book and are Paleo staples you'll want to have on hand.

Coconut milk: Opt for full-fat, often found in cans.

Cooking fats: Extra-virgin olive oil, avocado oil, coconut oil, and grass-fed ghee.

Spices: Spices elevate your cooking to the next level. Sea salt and freshly ground black pepper appear in nearly every recipe. Other frequently used spices include cinnamon, thyme, chili powder, onion powder, garlic powder, cumin, Italian seasoning, oregano, and paprika.

Broth: Chicken, beef, and vegetable broth can be used interchangeably in most recipes. For the most nutrition, make your own gut-healing bone broth (page 40) and use it in place of other types of broth.

Apple cider vinegar: A common vinegar used in Paleo cooking.

Coconut aminos: A replacement for soy sauce.

Tapioca flour or arrowroot flour: A replacement for wheat and corn flours to thicken sauces and soups.

Meat: Ground beef and pork, chuck roast, chicken breasts and thighs, frozen fish.

Vegetables: Onions, garlic, celery, carrots, and sweet potatoes.

Eggs: For breakfast recipes. Also, hard-boiled eggs make a great grab-and-go snack.

Snack foods: Fresh berries, nut butters, nuts and seeds, olives, and beef jerky.

Skip

It's all too easy to fall off the wagon when temptation is staring at you from the pantry. Consider removing all non-Paleo items from your house and donating them. Here are items to clear out:

Dairy: Milk, cheese, ice cream, yogurt, etc.

Grains: Breads, pastas, pastries, cereals, granola bars, crackers, chips, popcorn, oatmeal, etc.

Beans: Hummus, soy sauce, tofu, peanut butter and peanuts, etc.

Artificial foods: Margarine and other butter substitutes, egg replacements, anything with an ingredient you can't pronounce or don't recognize!

Sugar: Candy, all sweeteners except natural ones.

Sweet drinks: Fruit juice, energy drinks, sweetened teas, soda, etc.

Appliances Beyond the Instant Pot

A few kitchen tools can seriously expedite your food preparation.

Sharp chef's knife and cutting board: Absolute must-haves!

Spiralizer or vegetable peeler: Can be used to make vegetable noodles.

Food processor: Speeds up the process of chopping, grating, mixing, and slicing your ingredients.

Box grater: Can be used to make riced cauliflower.

Immersion blender: Great for blending soups and sauces in the Instant Pot (a regular standing blender works, too).

Trivet: A circular rack or steamer basket placed at the bottom of the inner bowl of your Instant Pot.

Heatproof dish: Find one that fits inside of your pot.

Silicone gloves or mitts: Make removing your dish safe and easy.

Vacuum sealer: Great for packaging your leftovers for the freezer.

PALEO IN YOUR INSTANT POT: A PERFECT FIT

I won't sugarcoat things (because sugar certainly isn't Paleo!): Eating Paleo can lead to spending a lot of time in the kitchen. The Instant Pot is Paleo's perfect companion for this reason and many more.

Saves time and energy: Foods are cooked much faster with an Instant Pot compared to other types of cooking methods. The steam created transmits heat to food four times faster than boiling!

Preserves nutrients: Studies show that nutrients and antioxidants are better preserved by pressure cooking. Vitamins and minerals are not leached away by water, as they are when boiled.

Easier to digest: Research indicates that pressure-cooked foods are easier to digest and extract nutrition from. Pressure cooking also deactivates some anti-nutrients.

Kills bacteria: The high heat in the Instant Pot rapidly kills microorganisms present in food, even killing types of bacteria that can survive at boiling levels. This quality makes the Instant Pot effective at sterilizing jam jars, glass baby bottles, and even water.

Less mess: Instant Pot meals are one-pot meals, which means less cleanup in the kitchen after cooking.

Set and forget: Instant Pot cooking is as simple as pressing a button and walking away.

About the Recipes

This book includes 75 Paleo Instant Pot recipes that are easy to prepare and use affordable everyday ingredients. You'll find full meals, but some of the meat dishes will need a vegetable dish prepared alongside, and vice versa. We've highlighted recipes that are nut-free, vegan, and vegetarian for your quick reference. You'll also find several tips for making the recipes easier and swaps to make them work best for you. Just follow the simple instructions and you'll be cooking up a Paleo storm in no time!

In the next chapter, we'll be talking all about the Instant Pot. If you're an Instant Pot pro, feel free to skip it; if not, get ready to learn how this one-pot wonder will take your cooking to the next level!

Bone Broth in an Instant, page 40

CHAPTER 2

Getting to Know Your Instant Pot

Now that you know about the health-optimizing effects of the Paleo diet, we'd like to introduce you to the Instant Pot, which makes cooking delicious Paleo foods a breeze. The Instant Pot is a multicooker that pressure cooks, slow cooks, and even makes Paleo-friendly yogurt! It uses pressure to force steam and moisture into food, which shortens cooking time, improves digestibility, and preserves more nutrients and antioxidants than other cooking methods such as boiling and roasting. In this chapter, you'll learn all the Instant Pot basics: safety features and functions, how and when to release the pressure, adjusting for altitude, cleaning, and care. Let's get going!

Instant Friends with Your Multicooker

Eating a real-food diet in a processed-food world presents challenges, and one of the most formidable is feeling overwhelmed in the kitchen. Even seasoned pros struggle with preparing enough food to stay the Paleo course. That's why we were thrilled to discover the Instant Pot! It revolutionized cooking by making it easy to whip up amazing Paleo meals that our families love. Pressure-cooking with the Instant Pot is as simple as placing your ingredients inside, sealing the lid, pushing a button, and walking away! Plus, there's hardly any cleanup: Pressure cooking, slow cooking, sautéing, browning, steaming, and simmering are all done in the same pot, so there's no pile of dirty cookware waiting for you after the meal.

In this chapter, you'll learn how easy it is to use your Instant Pot and make the most of its multifunctionality. Even if you're an Instant Pot pro, we recommend that you hang on for a refresher. Or feel free to skip to the recipes and get cooking!

Different Pressure Cookers

The recipes in this book are designed for the most popular version of the Instant Pot, the 6-quart IP-Duo60. Other models are similar, and all the recipes easily adapt to any version. Be sure to always follow the manufacturer's instructions in your owner's manual.

SCALING DOWN FOR THE IP MINI

If you're cooking for fewer than four people, have limited counter space, or prepare smaller meals and side dishes often, the 3-quart Instant Pot Mini is for you! The IP Mini has all the same functions as the 6-quart models, and cooks your food under the same amount of pressure in the same amount of time. To scale recipes down for the IP Mini, simply cut the recipe ingredient quantities in half and use a minimum liquid amount of ½ cup. For instance, if a 6-quart IP recipe includes a pound of meat and 1 cup water, you'll use ½ pound of meat and ½ cup of water in the IP mini. A perk of using less liquid is that your IP Mini will take less time to pressurize. When you're cooking food that absorbs a lot of liquid, such as chia seeds, ensure the ratio of liquid to absorbing ingredient stays the same.

The Anatomy of an Instant Pot

Unlike the risky and dangerous pressure cookers of the past, the Instant Pot is a reliable and safe pressure cooker, as well as a slow cooker, steamer, poacher, and sauté pan. We want you to feel completely comfortable with your Instant Pot, so it's time to get close and personal with your new countertop cooker and familiarize yourself with all its parts and accessories.

LID

The lid locks into the Instant Pot base. It contains several components that facilitate easy and safe pressure cooking, including the steam release valve, the float valve, and the sealing ring. The two tabs on the lid fit into the holes in the handles on either side of your Instant Pot to save counter space when using the sauté function without the lid. All the lid components are removable and function optimally when cleaned regularly with warm soapy water.

STEAM RELEASE VALVE

The small loose handle on the top of the lid is the steam release valve. It can move between two positions, Sealing and Venting, and controls whether the pressure is sealed in the pot or released, respectively. See the "Safety First" section (page 23) to learn how to release steam from your Instant Pot safely.

FLOAT VALVE

The float valve is a small button on the lid that acts as a safety feature. When your Instant Pot comes to pressure, the float valve pops up and locks the lid, preventing it from being opened during pressure cooking. Only when the pressure is fully released will the float valve fall back into place and unlock the lid.

RING

The silicone sealing ring sits inside the lid's perimeter and makes it possible for the lid to seal shut when under pressure. It tends to pick up cooking odors, so you'll want to wash it after every use. It's recommended to replace your sealing ring every 6 to 18 months due to discoloration, odors, and general wear and tear.

ANTI-BLOCK SHIELD

The anti-block shield is the small metal cap that snaps into place directly below the steam release valve on the lid's underside. Its purpose is to block food from clogging the vent.

INNER POT

Depending on your model, the removable stainless-steel inner pot has either a Max line near the top or PC Max—⅔ and ½ lines. Never overfill the inner pot because this can clog up the float and steam release valves, create safety issues, and compromise performance. If your Instant Pot has a Max line, it's fine to fill it to this point when slow cooking but *not* when pressure cooking or cooking foods that expand such as rice, beans, and Paleo-friendly chia seeds. Fill the inner pot two-thirds full for pressure cooking and half full for foods that expand or foam up when cooked, such as applesauce and starchy porridges.

OUTER POT

The outer pot houses all the digital components of your Instant Pot. The control panel consists of buttons that allow you to choose functions and settings for different types of foods, adjust pressure, set cook times, and more. Never submerge the outer pot in water. To clean, simply wipe down with a damp cloth.

STEAMER RACK

Your Instant Pot comes with a stainless-steel steamer rack designed to hold foods above the liquid added to the pot. There are many metal and silicone racks, baskets, and accessories available in stores and online to fit your every Instant Pot cooking need.

CONDENSATION COLLECTOR

Condensation sometimes collects and drips from the lid of your Instant Pot during cooking. The small plastic container that comes with your Instant Pot hooks onto the outside of the pot just under the lid and collects this moisture before it can drip onto your countertop. It's a good idea to remove and clean your condensation collector frequently.

PLASTIC RICE PADDLE AND SOUP SPOON

Included in your Instant Pot are a plastic rice paddle and soup spoon. These are handy utensils, even if you use them to remove foods other than rice and soup, and won't scratch your stainless-steel inner pot.

MEASURING CUP

The 160ml cup that comes with your Instant Pot is intended for measuring rice. Unless you're cooking rice for someone not on the Paleo diet, store it away for another use.

THE ROLE OF LIQUID

It's essential to have at least 1 cup of liquid in the pot when pressure cooking, or there won't be enough steam produced for the pot to pressurize. If this happens, you may see a BURN message on your display, indicating that the inner pot became too hot and the cooking process was suspended. This is easily fixed, and you can get back to cooking your meal. Thin out thick liquids with more water, make sure the steam release valve is set to Sealing, check that the silicone ring is fitted properly in the lid and that the lid components are free of debris, and ensure that the lid is closed correctly.

Instant Pot Functions

Each button on your Instant pot activates a function. In this section, we will explore each of them. The recipes in this book are designed for beginners, so you'll primarily use the Pressure Cook or Manual button on your Instant Pot. Many recipes also use the Sauté button to sear meat or sauté onions and garlic before pressure cooking. When it's time to release the pressure, you'll see both Natural Release or Quick Release, or a combination of the two.

The LCD Display

The LCD display informs you of each stage of the cooking process. In the standby state, the display reads OFF. After choosing a function and cook time, there will be a 10-second delay before cooking begins. As the pot heats up, the word ON will show until the pot comes to pressure. When the working pressure is reached, the display will change to the cook time and begin a countdown, indicating the remaining time in minutes.

The Functions

The control panel is where you'll find all the buttons you need to control every aspect of your Instant Pot. All the models have the same basic functions; however, the displays and button names vary.

PRESSURE COOK/MANUAL
Depending on your model, the Pressure Cook or Manual button is an all-purpose pressure-cooking setting. You can cook just about any Paleo recipe on this setting because it allows you to easily customize the pressure and cook times. The Pressure Cook/Manual setting defaults to High Pressure, but you can switch between High and Low Pressure using the Pressure Level or Pressure button. Use the + and - buttons to adjust the cooking time. If your model has a dial, this is how you customize the preset programs, time, and temperature.

QUICK COOK SETTINGS
The following Smart Programs are highlighted because you are most likely to use them for cooking Paleo. These preset buttons are programmed with predetermined pressure and cook times that vary slightly between models. This makes cooking easy if you're not following a recipe.

Soup/Broth: Simmer gut-healing soups and broths on this setting that increases heat levels slowly and gradually.

Meat/Stew: This is best for cooking large cuts of meat at high pressure and all types of stews. When cooking meat, use the Less mode for a soft texture, Normal mode for very tender meat, and More mode for fall-off-the-bone tenderness. Keep in mind that if starting with a frozen block of meat, the recipe cook time may need to be increased by 50 percent or more.

Bean/Chili: Use this program for your favorite Paleo-friendly chili recipes.

Poultry: If your model has this button, the pot will default to high pressure to quickly cook chicken, turkey, duck, or wild poultry.

Steam: If your model has a Steam button, be sure to use a steamer basket or trivet to raise foods off the pot's bottom. Under a fast and steep pressure build, the Steam program will quickly cook vegetables or fish and reheat food.

SAUTÉ

You'll find the Sauté function used in many recipes because it turns your Instant Pot into a pan, allowing you to sauté, simmer, and sear foods before cooking. Bonus: fewer dirty dishes! Change the heat level from Normal to Less or More by pressing the Sauté button multiple times (or on older models, the Adjust button). Use a tempered glass lid to speed up the cooking process. When using the Sauté function, the word HOT will display when working heat is reached. We recommend that you add oil and start sautéing before HOT appears.

SLOW COOK

Slow cook your favorite recipes without pressure. Select the Slow Cook button and use the + and - buttons to set the time. You can change the temperature to Less, Normal, or More, which corresponds to warm, low, and high settings on traditional slow cookers. Cover with the Instant Pot lid, leaving the vent open, or use a tempered glass lid.

DELAY START/TIMER

The Delay Start or Timer button, depending on your model, allows you to program a delayed start for all functions except Sauté, Yogurt, and Keep Warm. After selecting your cooking program and adjusting the time as needed, press Delay Start/Timer, then use the + and - buttons to set the delayed hours and minutes.

KEEP WARM/CANCEL

You will either have a combined Keep Warm/Cancel function, or it will be two separate buttons. When cooking is complete, your Instant Pot switches to Keep Warm and holds your food at 140°F for up to 10 hours, allowing you freedom from the cooking process during the day or overnight. Unlike the cooking countdown, when Keep Warm activates, the timer counts upward by minutes. You can also press Keep Warm/Cancel to cancel any cooking program.

Other Functions

Your Instant Pot may come with other preset functions that may or may not be applicable to your Paleo diet. The Rice, Multigrain, and Porridge buttons are preset pressure cook programs that you're unlikely to use. However, if you choose to cook these foods, use Rice for white rice, Multigrain for brown rice and other grains, and Porridge for oatmeal and starchy porridges. Additionally, you can use the Yogurt function to make Paleo yogurt from nondairy milk. If your model has a Sous Vide, Cake, Egg, or Sterilize button, check your user manual for directions.

ADJUSTING FOR ALTITUDE

If you live at 3,000 feet or more above sea level, you'll have to adjust the pressure cook times for your recipes since, at these heights, water boils at a lower temperature, and it'll take a little longer for your food to cook. It's recommended that you increase the cooking time by 5 percent for every 1,000 feet above 2,000 feet. For example, a 20-minute pressure cook time would change to 21 minutes at 3,000 feet, 22 minutes at 4,000 feet, 23 minutes at 5,000 feet, and so on.

Releasing Pressure

The float valve drops and the cover unlocks when pressure has released after cooking. During a natural release, the pressure comes down on its own. This usually happens in 15 to 20 minutes. Applying a cold, damp towel over the cover of your Instant Pot accelerates the process. During a quick release, your pot depressurizes in 1 to 2 minutes. After cooking, carefully move the steam release valve from Sealing to Venting, keeping your hands and face away from the valve opening. Quick release is not recommended if the pot is full or for starchy liquids that can spatter out with the steam and clog the vent. See the "Safety First" section (page 23) for more information.

Instant Pot from Start to Finish

Now that you're familiar with all the nuts and bolts of your Instant Pot, let's review how to cook a Paleo recipe to perfection from start to finish!

1. Place the inner pot inside the Instant Pot and plug it in. The word OFF will light up on the display panel when the cooker is connected and on standby.

2. If browning, sautéing, or simmering ingredients, select Sauté, and add the ingredients. Press Cancel or Keep Warm/Cancel, depending on your model, to stop the Sauté function.

3. Once it's time to pressure cook, place the desired ingredients in the pot, including a minimum of 1 cup of liquid if your recipe doesn't provide enough from wet ingredients, such as the liquid in tomatoes. Secure the lid and move the steam release valve to the Sealing position.

4. Select Pressure Cook or Manual, depending on your model. If desired, change the pressure level from high to low using the Pressure Level or Pressure button. Use the + and - buttons to set the time. If you choose a preset program, press the preset button or the Adjust button to change the mode from Normal to Less or More, if desired. A few seconds after the cook time has been entered, the cooker will automatically start, and the word ON will light up on the display.

5. After preheating for about 10 minutes, or longer if there is a lot of food, the pot will fully come to pressure. The float valve will pop up, and the digital display will start counting down the entered cook time.

6. Once cooking is complete, use a natural or quick release. Press Cancel if you don't want the Keep Warm mode to activate. Carefully remove the lid.

7. To reduce and thicken the liquid in a dish, select Sauté and simmer to the desired consistency. Press Cancel and serve.

8. Turn off your Instant Pot by unplugging it.

Cleaning Your Instant Pot

Unplug your Instant Pot and let it cool down before cleaning. The inner pot is dishwasher safe; however, hand wash it to prevent "rainbow" discoloration of the stainless steel. The anti-block shield, steam release valve, and sealing ring can all be removed from the lid and cleaned. The lid can be hand washed and the outer heating unit wiped down with a damp cloth.

Now let's get cooking!

CHAPTER 3

Breakfast

Hard- and Soft-Boiled Eggs 28

< Green Veggie Frittata 29

Eggs in Purgatory 30

Spicy Sausage and "No-tato" Hash 31

"Cheesy" Bacon and Eggs 32

Coconut-Blueberry Chia Porridge 33

Sweet Potato Breakfast Bowls 34

Grain-Free Bircher Bowls with Yogurt 35

Hard- and Soft-Boiled Eggs

MAKES 1 OR MORE EGGS (YOUR CHOICE)

PREP TIME: 1 minute

PRESSURE BUILD: 5 to 10 minutes

COOK TIME: 2 minutes (soft-boiled) or 5 minutes (hard-boiled), High Pressure

PRESSURE RELEASE: 1 to 5 minutes, Natural then Quick

TOTAL TIME: 9 to 21 minutes

VEGETARIAN, NUT-FREE, UNDER 30 MINUTES

The Instant Pot perfectly pressure cooks incredible egg edibles every time. In a few minutes, you'll be feasting on the heavenly tender whites and firm yolks of hard-boiled eggs or the delectable custardy whites and runny yolks of soft-boiled eggs.

1 or more large eggs

1. Pour 1 cup of water into the bowl of the Instant Pot. Place a trivet, steamer basket, or silicone egg rack on the bottom. Place the eggs on the trivet. It's okay if they touch, and you can even stack them.

2. Secure the lid and seal the vent. Select Pressure Cook or Manual and cook on high pressure for 2 minutes for soft-boiled eggs or 5 minutes for hard-boiled eggs (or 6 minutes if you want firmer yolks). Allow the pressure to naturally release for 1 minute for soft-boiled eggs or 5 minutes for hard-boiled eggs, then quick release the remaining pressure in the pot and remove the lid.

3. Meanwhile, fill a large bowl with ice and cold water.

4. With a slotted spoon, transfer the eggs to the ice bath. This will stop the cooking.

5. Peel, eat, and enjoy!

TIP: To make poached eggs, follow step 1, then grease heatproof or silicone egg poaching cups with avocado oil, crack an egg into each cup, and place the cups on the trivet. Cook on low pressure for 3 minutes, then quick release. If the eggs are not set to your liking, cook for an additional 1 to 2 minutes.

PER SERVING: Calories: 78; Total fat: 5g; Sodium: 62mg: Carbohydrates: 1g; Sugars: 1g; Protein: 6g

Green Veggie Frittata

SERVES 4
PREP TIME: 10 minutes
PRESSURE BUILD: 5 to 10 minutes

COOK TIME: 12 minutes, High Pressure
PRESSURE RELEASE: 15 minutes, Natural then Quick

TOTAL TIME: 42 to 47 minutes

VEGETARIAN, UNDER AN HOUR

Frittatas are open-faced omelets that are quick to whip up and make a stunning presentation on your breakfast table. This veggie frittata features green vegetables, but you can swap in any color of bell pepper or onion that you prefer. There are virtually endless combinations of ingredients that you can use in this versatile recipe; add sautéed ground meats, sausage, and more!

1 tablespoon coconut oil or ghee

8 eggs

⅓ cup coconut cream or full-fat coconut milk

½ teaspoon sea salt

½ teaspoon freshly ground black pepper

½ teaspoon chili powder

¼ cup green bell pepper, diced

3 scallions, both white and green parts, chopped

½ cup packed fresh baby spinach

1 large avocado, sliced

1. Grease the bottom and sides of a 6- or 7-inch heatproof dish that fits in the bowl of your Instant Pot with the oil. Set aside.

2. In a medium bowl or food processor, whisk together the eggs, coconut cream, salt, black pepper, and chili powder until fluffy. Add the bell pepper, scallions, and spinach. Stir to combine. Pour the mixture into the prepared dish and cover with foil.

3. Pour 1½ cups of water into the bowl of the Instant Pot. Place a trivet in the bottom of the pot. Place the dish containing the frittata on the trivet.

4. Secure the lid and seal the vent. Select Pressure Cook or Manual and cook on high pressure for 12 minutes, then allow the pressure to naturally release for 15 minutes. Quick release the remaining pressure in the pot and remove the lid. If not done to your liking, cook for an additional 5 minutes at high pressure, followed by a quick release.

5. When cool enough to handle, top with avocado slices to serve.

TIP: You can also use a springform pan for this recipe. Wrap the bottom with foil to prevent leakage.

PER SERVING: Calories: 302; Total fat: 24g; Sodium: 424mg; Carbohydrates: 10g; Sugars: 4g; Protein: 14g

Eggs in Purgatory

SERVES 4
PREP TIME: 5 minutes
PRESSURE BUILD: 5 to 10 minutes

COOK TIME: 21 minutes, Sauté/High Pressure
PRESSURE RELEASE: Quick

TOTAL TIME: 31 to 36 minutes

VEGETARIAN, NUT-FREE, UNDER AN HOUR

Eggs simmering in bubbly red broth are a recipe for gustatory heaven. Also known as *shakshuka*, the eggplant in this version results in a "meatier" texture, and harissa or paprika intensifies the smoky, rich sauce.

2 tablespoons extra-virgin olive oil
1 small eggplant, cut into ½-inch pieces
3 large garlic cloves, minced

1 (28-ounce) can diced tomatoes, with most of the liquid drained out
1 tablespoon harissa or 1 teaspoon smoked paprika
¼ teaspoon red pepper flakes
½ teaspoon sea salt

¼ teaspoon freshly ground black pepper
4 to 6 eggs
1 tablespoon chopped fresh parsley (optional)
Hot sauce (optional)

1. Select Sauté on the Instant Pot. Heat the oil until it shimmers.

2. Sauté the eggplant until it starts to soften, about 4 minutes. Add the garlic and cook for 1 minute more.

3. Add the tomatoes, harissa, red pepper flakes, salt, and black pepper.

4. Secure the lid and seal the vent. Select Pressure Cook or Manual and cook on high pressure for 10 minutes, then quick release the pressure in the pot. Press Cancel and remove the lid.

5. Select Sauté and stir the sauce. Into a small bowl, crack one egg at a time. Lower each egg into the pot and gently pour it out of the bowl onto the sauce.

6. Simmer until the eggs are set but the yolks are runny, 4 to 6 minutes. Covering with a lid will speed up the process.

7. Top with the parsley and hot sauce (if using).

TIP: Harissa is a North African hot chile pepper paste or seasoning. It can be found in the international section of the grocery store or at Middle Eastern markets.

PER SERVING: Calories: 219; Total fat: 12g; Sodium: 737mg; Carbohydrates: 19g; Sugars: 10g; Protein: 9g

Spicy Sausage and "No-tato" Hash

SERVES 4
PREP TIME: 10 minutes
PRESSURE BUILD: 10 to 20 minutes

COOK TIME: 15 minutes, Sauté/High Pressure
PRESSURE RELEASE: 10 minutes, Natural then Quick

TOTAL TIME: 45 to 55 minutes

NUT-FREE, UNDER AN HOUR

Hashes originated as a way to use up leftovers. The "hasheries" of old left no ingredient to disuse, and creative cooks turned whatever foodstuffs they had into dishes of great synchronicity. These days, hash isn't always about leftovers, but it can be. Your Instant Pot practically cooks this flavorful chorizo and sweet potato hash itself.

1 tablespoon extra-virgin olive oil
16 ounces uncooked chorizo
2 garlic cloves, minced
1 yellow onion, diced

½ teaspoon dried rosemary
1 cup chicken broth
3 medium sweet potatoes, peeled and cut into bite-size pieces

½ teaspoon freshly ground black pepper
1 tablespoon balsamic vinegar

1. Select Sauté on the Instant Pot. Heat the oil until it shimmers.

2. Sauté the chorizo, garlic, onion, and rosemary for 3 to 5 minutes until browned, stirring occasionally. Press Cancel.

3. Pour the broth into the pot. Use a wooden spoon to scrape up any pieces of food stuck to the bottom. Add the sweet potatoes to the pot and stir to combine.

4. Secure the lid and seal the vent. Select Pressure Cook or Manual and cook on high pressure for 10 minutes, then allow the pressure to naturally release for 10 minutes. Quick release any remaining pressure in the pot and remove the lid.

5. Stir in the pepper and vinegar and enjoy.

TIP: Chorizo is a highly seasoned sausage that's usually made from pork or beef. Mexican chorizo is a raw, ground product and Spanish chorizo is cooked. You can use either type in this recipe. Be sure to read the ingredient list, as many types of store-bought chorizo contain non-Paleo ingredients.

PER SERVING: Calories: 471; Total fat: 32g; Sodium: 1,181mg: Carbohydrates: 28g; Sugars: 9g; Protein: 18g

"Cheesy" Bacon and Eggs

SERVES 4
PREP TIME: 5 minutes
PRESSURE BUILD: 5 to 10 minutes

COOK TIME: 33 minutes, Sauté/High Pressure
PRESSURE RELEASE: Quick

TOTAL TIME: 43 to 48 minutes

UNDER AN HOUR

Bacon and eggs are the quintessential Paleo breakfast, and this recipe takes the classic combination to new heights! Nutritional yeast creates a dairy-free cheese in this easy egg bake that's packed with healthy fats and lots of flavor.

1 tablespoon coconut oil or ghee
6 slices bacon, diced
6 large eggs

¼ cup full-fat coconut milk
¼ cup nutritional yeast
¼ teaspoon sea salt

¼ teaspoon freshly ground black pepper
2 cups fresh kale leaves, chopped

1. Grease the bottom and sides of a 6- or 7-inch heatproof dish that fits inside the bowl of your Instant Pot with the ghee. Set aside.

2. Select Sauté on the Instant Pot. Cook the bacon until crispy, 5 to 8 minutes.

3. Meanwhile, in a medium bowl, whisk the eggs with the coconut milk, nutritional yeast, salt, and pepper. Set aside.

4. Stir the kale into the bacon. Press Cancel.

5. Pour the egg mixture into the prepared baking dish and, using a slotted spoon, add the bacon and kale. Cover with foil.

6. Place a trivet into the bowl and add 1½ cups of water. Place the dish containing the egg mixture onto the trivet.

7. Secure the lid and seal the vent. Select Pressure Cook or Manual and cook on high pressure for 20 minutes, then quick release the pressure in the pot and remove the lid. Depending on the depth of your dish, you may need an additional 5 or more minutes of cook time.

8. Remove the egg bake from the Instant Pot. Cut into pieces and serve.

TIP: You can remove the excess bacon fat from the pot in step 5 and save it for future use.

PER SERVING: Calories: 260; Total fat: 19g; Sodium: 451mg: Carbohydrates: 5g; Sugars: 2g; Protein: 18g

Coconut-Blueberry Chia Porridge

SERVES 4 TO 6
PREP TIME: 5 minutes
PRESSURE BUILD: 5 to 10 minutes

COOK TIME: 5 minutes, High Pressure
PRESSURE RELEASE: 5 minutes Natural then Quick

TOTAL TIME: 20 to 25 minutes

VEGAN, UNDER 30 MINUTES

This healthy Paleo porridge whips up in minutes and is especially nice on those days when you prefer an alternative to eggs. Chia seeds are chock-full of omega-3 fatty acids, amino acids, calcium, and disease-fighting antioxidants. Chia's abundance of soluble fiber makes it handy when you want a grain-free recipe to gel, such as porridge. You can use any fresh berries you have on hand and adjust the amount of maple syrup to your liking.

1 (14-ounce) can full-fat coconut milk
½ cup chia seeds
½ cup any type of nut, or a mix

¼ cup pumpkin seeds
¼ cup pure maple syrup or raw honey
½ teaspoon ground cinnamon

½ teaspoon pure vanilla extract
2 cups fresh blueberries

1. Pour 1½ cups of water into the bowl of the Instant Pot. Place a trivet in the pot.

2. In a heatproof bowl or dish that fits inside the bowl of your Instant Pot, combine the coconut milk, chia seeds, nuts, pumpkin seeds, maple syrup, cinnamon, vanilla, and ½ cup of water. Stir in the blueberries and place the bowl on the trivet.

3. Secure the lid and seal the vent. Select Pressure Cook or Manual and cook on high pressure for 5 minutes, then allow the pressure to naturally release for 5 minutes. Quick release any remaining pressure in the pot and remove the lid. The porridge will thicken as it cools.

TIP: For a nut-free version, substitute your favorite seeds, or add more fruit such as diced apples and pears.

PER SERVING: Calories: 530; Total fat: 37g; Sodium: 18mg: Carbohydrates: 43g; Sugars: 24g; Protein: 13g

Sweet Potato Breakfast Bowls

SERVES 2

PREP TIME: 5 minutes

PRESSURE BUILD: 5 to
10 minutes

COOK TIME: 6 minutes, High
Pressure

PRESSURE RELEASE:
10 minutes, Natural
then Quick

TOTAL TIME: 26 to 31 minutes

VEGAN, UNDER AN HOUR

This blend of tubers, fruit, nuts, and spices is a grain-free Paleo divinity. Not only is it better for your health to ditch the gluten, phytates, and lectins found in grains, we would argue that it's tastier for your palate, too! Use any variety of sweet potato from orange to white to purple and swap in sunflower seed butter, which tastes like peanut butter, to make it nut-free.

1 sweet potato, peeled
    and chopped

1 apple or pear, cored
    and chopped

½ cup nondairy milk

2 tablespoons nut or seed
    butter (almond, cashew,
    sunflower)

¼ teaspoon ground cinnamon

Pinch ground nutmeg

1. In a 6-or 7-inch heatproof dish that fits inside the bowl of your Instant Pot, combine the sweet potatoes and apples.

2. Put a trivet in the pot and pour in 1½ cups of water. Set the dish on the trivet. Secure the lid and seal the vent. Select Pressure Cook or Manual and cook on high pressure for 6 minutes, then allow the pressure to naturally release for 10 minutes. Quick release any remaining pressure in the pot and remove the lid.

3. Add the milk, nut butter, cinnamon, and nutmeg to the bowl. Use an immersion or regular blender to combine, or leave chunky. Add more milk if needed. Serve hot in bowls.

TIP: Top with crunchy chopped fresh apples, slivered almonds, pumpkin seeds, or grain-free granola.

PER SERVING: Calories: 209; Total fat: 9g; Sodium: 81mg: Carbohydrates: 30g; Sugars: 13g; Protein: 5g

Grain-Free Bircher Bowls with Yogurt

SERVES 4 TO 6
PREP TIME: 5 minutes
PRESSURE BUILD: 5 to 10 minutes

COOK TIME: 3 minutes, High Pressure
PRESSURE RELEASE: Quick

TOTAL TIME: 13 to 18 minutes

VEGAN, UNDER 30 MINUTES

In this recipe developed at the turn of the 20th century by Swiss physician Maximilian Bircher-Benner, grains such as oats were soaked overnight in milk or juice, topped with fruit, and served for breakfast. In this Paleo rendition, there's no overnight soaking—seeds replace the oats and are pressure cooked with a touch of sweetness, then served over yogurt. Choose coconut, cashew, or almond milk yogurt to keep your Bircher bowls dairy-free.

¼ cup unsalted pumpkin seeds

¼ cup unsalted sunflower seeds

¼ cup chia seeds

2 apples, cored and cut into bite-size pieces

1 cup unsweetened almond or coconut milk

1 teaspoon pure vanilla extract

½ teaspoon ground cinnamon

¼ cup pure maple syrup (optional)

1 (32-ounce) container nondairy yogurt

1. In the bowl of the Instant Pot, combine the pumpkin seeds, sunflower seeds, chia seeds, apples, almond milk, vanilla, and cinnamon.

2. Secure the lid and seal the vent. Select Pressure Cook or Manual and cook on high pressure for 3 minutes, then quick release the pressure in the pot and remove the lid. Stir in the maple syrup (if using).

3. Serve the warm seed mixture over the nondairy yogurt in individual bowls.

TIP: You can use whatever chopped nuts or seeds you like or have on hand.

PER SERVING: Calories: 378; Total fat: 20g; Sodium: 92mg: Carbohydrates: 48g; Sugars: 25g; Protein: 7g

CHAPTER 4

Soups and Stews

Beef Goulash 38

Creamy Butternut Soup 39

Bone Broth in an Instant 40

< Pumpkin Soup with Fennel and Leeks 41

Sweet Potato and "Pea-not" Stew 42

Chicken Taco Soup 43

Chicken "Pozole" Verde 44

Day-After-Thanksgiving Soup 45

Pork Green Chili 46

Pizza Soup 47

Beef Goulash

SERVES 6

PREP TIME: 10 minutes

PRESSURE BUILD: 10 to 20 minutes

COOK TIME: 34 Minutes, Sauté/High Pressure

PRESSURE RELEASE: 20 to 40 minutes, Natural

TOTAL TIME: 1 hour, 14 minutes to 1 hour, 44 minutes

NUT-FREE OPTION, WORTH THE WAIT

Traditional Hungarian goulash showcases paprika, the country's national spice. This dish highlights paprika, belonging to the same plant family as hot chiles, but from sweeter, less spicy varieties.

2 tablespoons extra-virgin olive oil, divided

1½ pounds beef chuck roast, trimmed of excess fat and cut into 1½-inch cubes

2 cups sliced onions

2 garlic cloves, minced

1½ teaspoons sea salt

¼ cup paprika

2 teaspoons caraway seeds

2 teaspoons dried marjoram or oregano

2 cups beef broth

1 (14-ounce) can diced tomatoes

2 large carrots, peeled and cut into 1-inch rounds

2 medium red bell peppers, cut into 1-inch pieces

1 large sweet potato, cut into 1-inch chunks

⅓ cup coconut cream (optional)

1. Select Sauté on the Instant Pot. Heat 1 tablespoon of oil until it shimmers.

2. Sauté the beef in batches until browned, about 5 minutes. Transfer to a plate and set aside. Add the remaining tablespoon of oil to the pot and sauté the onions and garlic with the salt for about 3 minutes until softened. Add the paprika, caraway seeds, and marjoram. Sauté for about 1 minute, or until fragrant.

3. Pour the broth into the pot and stir, using a wooden spoon to scrape off any bits stuck to the bottom of the pot. Return the beef to the pot and add the tomatoes with their juices, carrots, bell peppers, and sweet potato and stir to combine. Press Cancel.

4. Secure the lid and seal the vent. Select Pressure Cook or Manual and cook on high pressure for 25 minutes, then allow the pressure to release naturally and remove the lid.

5. Ladle into bowls and garnish with a dollop of coconut cream (if using).

TIP: The three most common types of paprika are sweet, hot, and smoked. This recipe and other recipes that call for "paprika" are referring to sweet paprika.

PER SERVING: Calories: 439; Total fat: 23g; Sodium: 1,107mg; Carbohydrates: 24g; Sugars: 9g; Protein: 35g

Creamy Butternut Soup

SERVES 4 TO 6
PREP TIME: 10 minutes
PRESSURE BUILD: 10 to 20 minutes

COOK TIME: 17 minutes, Sauté/High Pressure
PRESSURE RELEASE: 5 minutes, Natural then Quick

TOTAL TIME: 42 to 52 minutes

VEGAN, UNDER AN HOUR

The vivid, yellow-orange flesh of butternut squash has a sweet and slightly nutty flavor that is perfect for pureed soups. Hints of nutmeg and ginger round out the flavors to create a satisfying bowl you can enjoy any time of year. For extra nutrition, swap in Bone Broth in an Instant (page 40) for the vegetable broth.

1 tablespoon coconut oil

1 yellow onion, diced

1 tablespoon minced fresh garlic

1 tablespoon minced fresh ginger

1 butternut squash, peeled and cut into chunks (4 to 5 cups)

2 cups vegetable broth

1 cup full-fat coconut milk

1 teaspoon sea salt

½ teaspoon ground cinnamon

¼ teaspoon freshly ground black pepper

⅛ teaspoon ground nutmeg

1. Select Sauté on the Instant Pot. Heat the oil until it shimmers.

2. Add the onion, garlic, and ginger and sauté, stirring occasionally, about 2 minutes, until softened and translucent.

3. Add the squash, broth, coconut milk, salt, cinnamon, pepper, and nutmeg. Stir to combine. Press Cancel.

4. Secure the lid and seal the vent. Select Pressure Cook or Manual and cook on high pressure for 15 minutes, then allow the pressure to naturally release for 5 minutes. Quick release the remaining pressure in the pot and remove the lid.

5. Use an immersion blender to puree the soup, or let it cool slightly and transfer it to a regular blender in batches, making sure to vent the lid by removing the cap so steam can escape.

TIP: Always opt for organic full-fat coconut milk in a BPA-free can if possible. Many of the healthy fats are removed in "light" versions of coconut milk.

PER SERVING: Calories: 242; Total fat: 14g; Sodium: 885mg: Carbohydrates: 30g; Sugars: 9g; Protein: 3g

Bone Broth in an Instant

MAKES 8 CUPS
PREP TIME: 5 minutes
PRESSURE BUILD: 10 to 20 minutes

COOK TIME: 2 hours, Roast/High Pressure
PRESSURE RELEASE: 20 to 40 minutes, Natural

TOTAL TIME: 2 hours, 35 minutes to 3 hours, 5 minutes

NUT-FREE, WORTH THE WAIT

Bone broth is a staple of the Paleo diet touted for its gut-healing and immune-boosting benefits. It can be made from the bones of any type of animal. Bone broth is rich in collagen, gelatin, an array of minerals, and amino acids. It usually requires long hours of slow simmering on the stovetop; however, the Instant Pot speeds up this process to just a few hours. You get all the benefits in a fraction of the time!

2½ pounds beef bones, including short ribs, knuckles, oxtails, and more
1 teaspoon extra-virgin olive oil

1 yellow or white onion, quartered
2 celery stalks, quartered
1 carrot, quartered
4 garlic cloves, smashed

1 bay leaf
1 tablespoon apple cider vinegar
2 teaspoons sea salt

1. Preheat the oven to 400°F.

2. Toss the bones with the oil on a baking sheet and roast for 30 minutes.

3. Once cool enough to handle, combine the bones, onion, celery, carrot, garlic, bay leaf, vinegar, salt, and 8 cups of water in the bowl of the Instant Pot.

4. Secure the lid and seal the vent. Select Pressure Cook or Manual and cook on high pressure for 1½ hours, then allow the pressure to naturally release. Open the vent at the top and remove the lid. Press Cancel.

5. Carefully strain the broth using a fine-mesh strainer or cheesecloth. Store in the refrigerator for up to 1 week or in the freezer for up to 3 months.

TIP: You can also use a combination of animal bones (chicken, beef, pork, fish, etc.). A roasted chicken carcass makes for a delicious broth!

PER SERVING: Calories: 94; Total fat: 6g; Sodium: 607mg: Carbohydrates: 1g; Sugars: 1g; Protein: 8g

Pumpkin Soup with Fennel and Leeks

SERVES 4 TO 6
PREP TIME: 5 minutes
PRESSURE BUILD: 10 to 20 minutes

COOK TIME: 8 minutes, Sauté/High Pressure
PRESSURE RELEASE: 5 minutes, Natural then Quick

TOTAL TIME: 28 to 38 minutes

VEGAN, NUT-FREE, UNDER AN HOUR

With its large white bulb and green feathery top, fennel lends a mild anise flavor to dishes. When choosing fennel, pick ones with firm bulbs, bright green stalks, and fresh fronds. In this flavorful soup, the licorice flavor of fennel is balanced by garlic, smoked paprika, and other warming spices.

2 tablespoons extra-virgin olive oil
1 leek, white and light green parts only, thinly sliced
1 fennel bulb, fronds removed and thinly sliced

4 garlic cloves, coarsely chopped
2 teaspoons smoked paprika
½ teaspoon ground cumin
¼ teaspoon ground nutmeg
1 (15-ounce) can pumpkin puree

4 cups vegetable broth
1 teaspoon sea salt, plus more as needed
¼ teaspoon freshly ground black pepper, plus more as needed

1. Select Sauté on the Instant Pot. Heat the oil until it shimmers.

2. Add the leek, fennel, and garlic. Sauté for 2 to 3 minutes, until the vegetables start to soften. Press Cancel.

3. Add the paprika, cumin, nutmeg, pumpkin puree, broth, salt, and pepper, and stir to combine.

4. Secure the lid and seal the vent. Select Pressure Cook or Manual and cook on high pressure for 5 minutes, then allow the pressure to naturally release for 5 minutes. Quick release the remaining pressure in the pot and remove the lid. Press Cancel.

5. Taste and season with additional salt and pepper as needed. Serve and enjoy!

TIP: Ramp up the healthy fats in this soup by swapping in Bone Broth in an Instant (page 40) for the vegetable broth. Transform this into a creamy soup by adding in a can of full-fat coconut milk.

PER SERVING: Calories: 152; Total fat: 8g; Sodium: 1,197mg; Carbohydrates: 21g; Sugars: 9g; Protein: 3g

Sweet Potato and "Pea-not" Stew

SERVES 4 TO 6
PREP TIME: 5 minutes
PRESSURE BUILD: 10 to 20 minutes

COOK TIME: 9 minutes, Sauté/High Pressure
PRESSURE RELEASE: 5 minutes, Natural then Quick

TOTAL TIME: 29 to 39 minutes

VEGAN, UNDER AN HOUR

Peanut soup is traditional to West Africa and is a hearty mix of peanuts, sweet potatoes, hot spices, and beef. Despite the name, peanuts are classified as a legume and are not technically a nut. This thick and rich Paleo-friendly version substitutes sunflower seed butter for the peanuts and sturdy greens for the beef.

- 2 tablespoons coconut oil or extra-virgin olive oil
- 1 large yellow or white onion, diced
- 2 large sweet potatoes, peeled and cut into 1-inch chunks
- ⅓ cup sunflower seed butter
- 1 teaspoon smoked paprika
- ¼ teaspoon red pepper flakes or ⅛ teaspoon cayenne pepper
- 2 cups vegetable broth or water
- ½ teaspoon sea salt
- ¼ teaspoon freshly ground black pepper
- 1 to 2 cups coarsely chopped fresh spinach or kale

1. Select Sauté on the Instant Pot. Heat the oil until it shimmers.

2. Sauté the onion until softened, 2 to 3 minutes, stirring occasionally.

3. Add the sweet potatoes, sunflower seed butter, paprika, red pepper flakes, broth, salt, and black pepper. Stir to combine. Press Cancel.

4. Secure the lid and seal the vent. Select Pressure Cook or Manual and cook on high pressure for 6 minutes, then naturally release the pressure in the pot for 5 minutes. Quick release the remaining pressure in the pot and remove the lid.

5. Stir in the spinach to wilt. Serve and enjoy!

TIP: Add a can of diced fire-roasted tomatoes to impart a touch of tart sweetness.

PER SERVING: Calories: 305; Total fat: 19g; Sodium: 642mg: Carbohydrates: 31g; Sugars: 9g; Protein: 6g

Chicken Taco Soup

SERVES 4
PREP TIME: 5 minutes
PRESSURE BUILD: 10 to 20 minutes

COOK TIME: 15 minutes, High Pressure/Sauté
PRESSURE RELEASE: 10 minutes, Natural then Quick

TOTAL TIME: 40 to 50 minutes

UNDER AN HOUR

If it belongs in Paleo-friendly tacos, it works in Paleo-friendly taco soup! A distinctively Mexican-inspired blend of aromatic spices punctuates the chicken broth in this classic rendition. Coconut adds creamy undertones, while a topping of fresh cilantro, avocado, jalapeño, and lime brightens this bowl of broth.

- 1½ pounds boneless, skinless chicken breast or tenders
- 3 cups chicken broth
- 1 cup salsa
- 1½ teaspoons chili powder
- 1 teaspoon ground cumin
- ½ teaspoon paprika

- ½ teaspoon onion powder
- ½ teaspoon garlic powder
- 1 teaspoon sea salt
- ¼ teaspoon freshly ground black pepper
- 1 (14-ounce) can full-fat coconut cream or milk

- ½ cup chopped fresh cilantro
- 1 avocado, peeled, halved, pitted, and cut into slices
- 1 jalapeño pepper, cut into slices (optional)
- 1 lime, cut into wedges (optional)

1. In the bowl of the Instant Pot, combine the chicken, broth, salsa, chili powder, cumin, paprika, onion powder, garlic powder, salt, and pepper.

2. Secure the lid and seal the vent. Select Pressure Cook or Manual and cook on high pressure for 15 minutes, then allow the pressure to naturally release for 10 minutes. Quick release any remaining pressure in the pot and remove the lid. Press Cancel.

3. Remove the chicken and shred it with a fork. Set aside.

4. Select Sauté and whisk in the coconut cream.

5. Return the shredded chicken to the pot. Serve, topped with cilantro, avocado, jalapeño pepper (if using), and lime wedges (if using).

TIP: Full-fat coconut milk can be used in place of coconut cream. The soup should simmer on Sauté a little longer to reduce the broth, as coconut milk is thinner than coconut cream.

PER SERVING: Calories: 557; Total fat: 31g; Sodium: 1,959mg: Carbohydrates: 14g; Sugars: 7g; Protein: 57g

Chicken "Pozole" Verde

SERVES 4

PREP TIME: 10 minutes

PRESSURE BUILD: 10 to 20 minutes

COOK TIME: 24 minutes, Sauté/High Pressure

PRESSURE RELEASE: Quick

TOTAL TIME: 44 to 54 minutes

NUT-FREE, UNDER AN HOUR

Pozole is a traditional Mexican stew made with hominy, which is derived from corn. Often confused for a vegetable, corn is a member of the grain family, and thus not Paleo. In this recipe, cauliflower steps in as the perfect, more nutritious substitute.

1 yellow onion, quartered

1 pound fresh tomatillos, husked and coarsely chopped

1 poblano pepper, seeded and coarsely chopped

2 jalapeño peppers, seeded and coarsely chopped

1½ cup packed fresh cilantro, divided

3 garlic cloves, smashed

4 cups chicken broth, divided

2 tablespoons extra-virgin olive oil or lard

1 pound boneless, skinless chicken breast or thighs

1 tablespoon dried oregano

1 teaspoon ground cumin

½ teaspoon sea salt

¼ teaspoon freshly ground black pepper

1 head cauliflower, cut into small florets

4 radishes, thinly sliced

1 large avocado, diced

1 lime, cut into wedges

1. In a blender, blend the onion, tomatillos, poblano pepper, jalapeño peppers, ½ cup of cilantro, garlic, and 2 cups of broth until smooth. Set aside.

2. Select Sauté on the Instant Pot. Heat the oil until it shimmers, then sear the chicken until browned, about 2 minutes per side. Press Cancel.

3. Add the tomatillo mixture, the remaining 2 cups of broth, the oregano, cumin, salt, and black pepper to the bowl of the Instant Pot. Stir to combine.

4. Secure the lid and seal the vent. Select Pressure Cook or Manual and cook on high pressure for 15 minutes. Quick release the pressure in the pot and remove the lid. Press Cancel.

5. Remove the chicken to a cutting board. Set aside.

6. Select Sauté and add the cauliflower to the soup. Simmer for 5 minutes until softened. Meanwhile, shred the chicken with two forks and return it to the pot.

7. Garnish with radishes, avocado, remaining 1 cup of cilantro, and lime wedges.

PER SERVING: Calories: 400; Total fat: 20g; Sodium: 1,322mg: Carbohydrates: 28g; Sugars: 12g; Protein: 33g

Day-After-Thanksgiving Soup

SERVES 6

PREP TIME: 10 minutes

PRESSURE BUILD: 10 to 20 minutes

COOK TIME: 8 minutes, High Pressure

PRESSURE RELEASE: Quick

TOTAL TIME: 28 to 38 minutes

NUT-FREE, UNDER AN HOUR

Wondering what to do with all that leftover Thanksgiving turkey? In just minutes, your Instant Pot can make good use of it, as well as any side dishes you have left! Round out your holidays with this wonderfully nutritious, filling, easy meal you can make in a cinch. And it's not just for the holidays—this recipe is a great way to use up your meat and veggie leftovers all year long.

1 yellow or white onion, diced

3 garlic cloves, minced

2 large carrots, diced

2 large celery stalks, diced

1 zucchini, diced

1 large sweet potato, diced

2 tablespoons tomato paste

2 teaspoons Italian seasoning

2 cups cooked turkey
 meat, diced

5 cups turkey or
 chicken broth

1 teaspoon sea salt

½ teaspoon freshly ground
 black pepper

Chopped fresh flat-leaf
 parsley, for garnish
 (optional)

1. In the bowl of the Instant Pot, combine the onion, garlic, carrots, celery, zucchini, sweet potato, tomato paste, Italian seasoning, turkey meat, broth, salt, and pepper.

2. Secure the lid and seal the vent. Press Manual and cook on high pressure for 8 minutes, then quick release the pressure in the pot and remove the lid.

3. Garnish with fresh parsley (if using) and serve.

TIP: This soup is a good way to incorporate leftover vegetable sides from your holiday meal, such as green beans or sweet potatoes. Simply select Sauté after the cooking cycle is complete, stir in the cooked vegetables (preferably cut into bite-size pieces), and simmer until heated through.

PER SERVING: Calories: 176; Total fat: 3g; Sodium: 565mg: Carbohydrates: 14g; Sugars: 5g; Protein: 23g

Pork Green Chili

SERVES 4 TO 6
PREP TIME: 10 minutes
PRESSURE BUILD: 10 to 20 minutes

COOK TIME: 22 minutes, Sauté/High Pressure
PRESSURE RELEASE: Quick

TOTAL TIME: 42 to 52 minutes

NUT-FREE, UNDER AN HOUR

Fresh Hatch chiles can be found in late summer and early fall, or they can be purchased in jars or cans. You can also use two (7-ounce) cans of drained diced green chiles instead.

- 2 tablespoons extra-virgin olive oil or lard
- 2 pounds ground pork
- 1 yellow onion, diced
- 3 garlic cloves, minced
- ½ pound fresh tomatillos, husked and diced
- 1 jalapeño pepper, seeded and diced
- 2 cups roasted Hatch green chiles, diced
- 1 cup packed chopped fresh cilantro, divided
- 2 teaspoons ground cumin
- 1 teaspoon ground coriander
- 1 teaspoon dried oregano
- 2 cups chicken broth
- 1 teaspoon sea salt
- ¼ teaspoon freshly ground black pepper
- 1 zucchini, diced
- 2 limes, cut into wedges

1. Select Sauté on the Instant Pot. Heat the oil until it shimmers.

2. Sauté the pork for about 5 minutes, or until no longer pink. Add the onion and garlic and sauté 2 minutes until softened. Press Cancel.

3. Add the tomatillos, jalapeño pepper, chiles, ½ cup cilantro, cumin, coriander, oregano, broth, salt, and black pepper. Stir to combine.

4. Secure the lid and seal the vent. Select Pressure Cook or Manual and cook on high pressure for 10 minutes, then quick release the pressure in the pot and remove the lid. Press Cancel.

5. Select Sauté. Add the zucchini and simmer for 5 minutes, until soft.

6. Garnish with the remaining ½ cup cilantro and lime wedges and serve.

TIP: To roast fresh Hatch chiles, broil on a baking sheet until the skin is blistered and slightly blackened. Transfer to a bowl covered in plastic wrap for 10 minutes. Peel away the skin, remove the seeds and stems, then chop into smaller pieces.

PER SERVING: Calories: 741; Total fat: 56g; Sodium: 1,184mg: Carbohydrates: 25g; Sugars: 14g; Protein: 45g

Pizza Soup

SERVES 6
PREP TIME: 5 minutes
PRESSURE BUILD: 10 to
20 minutes

COOK TIME: 25 minutes,
Sauté/High Pressure
PRESSURE RELEASE: Quick

TOTAL TIME: 40 to 50 Minutes

NUT-FREE, UNDER AN HOUR

What do you do when you're craving pizza on your Paleo diet? You take your favorite pizza ingredients and toss them in a piquant bowl of broth! Sausage and pepperoni are perfectly Paleo when free of unwanted additives such as sugar and artificial preservatives. Serve with a fresh chopped vinaigrette salad for a winning combo.

1 tablespoon avocado oil
8 ounces ground beef, crumbled
8 ounces ground sausage, crumbled
2 ounces sliced uncured pepperoni
4 cups beef broth

4 cups sliced mushrooms
1 (14.5-ounce) can crushed tomatoes
1 (15-ounce) can tomato sauce
1 small onion, chopped
4 garlic cloves, minced

1 tablespoon Italian seasoning
½ teaspoon sea salt
½ teaspoon red pepper flakes (optional)
6 chopped fresh basil leaves (optional)

1. Select Sauté on the Instant Pot. Heat the oil until it shimmers.

2. Sauté the beef, sausage, and pepperoni for 5 minutes, or until the beef and sausage have browned. Drain the excess fat, if desired.

3. Add the broth, mushrooms, crushed tomatoes with their juices, tomato sauce, onion, garlic, Italian seasoning, salt, and red pepper flakes (if using). Press Cancel.

4. Secure the lid and seal the vent. Select Pressure Cook or Manual and cook on high pressure for 20 minutes, then quick release the pressure in the pot and remove the lid.

5. Garnish with basil (if using) and serve.

TIP: Convert this meal into a slow cooker recipe. Add all the ingredients to your slow cooker, stir to combine, cover, and cook on high heat for 3 to 4 hours, or low heat for 6 to 8 hours.

PER SERVING: Calories: 360; Total fat: 26g; Sodium: 1,722mg: Carbohydrates: 14g; Sugars: 7g; Protein: 19g

CHAPTER 5

Poultry Mains

Perfect Chicken Breast 50

Easy Chicken Fajitas 51

Chicken Cacciatore 52

Whole "Roasted" Chicken with Vegetables 53

< Herbed Chicken with Olives 54

Lemon Chicken 55

30-Minute Chile Chicken 56

Buffalo Chicken Wings 57

Cashew Chicken 58

Game-Day Chili 60

Turkey Bolognese 61

Duck with Mushrooms and Pearl Onions 62

Perfect Chicken Breast

SERVES 4 TO 6

PREP TIME: 1 minute

PRESSURE BUILD: 5 to
10 minutes

COOK TIME: 6 minutes, High
Pressure

PRESSURE RELEASE:
5 minutes, Natural
then Quick

TOTAL TIME: 17 to 22 minutes

**NUT-FREE, UNDER
30 MINUTES**

With the endless array of meals that you can add cooked chicken breast to, this recipe stands to be the most useful in your Paleo repertoire. As a tasty low-fat source of high-quality protein, chicken breast makes any meal more nutritious. Shred, chop, slice, or dice, then add to salads, casseroles, soups, stews, and more!

1 teaspoon sea salt

2 pounds boneless, skinless
chicken breast

1. Salt the chicken breast on both sides.

2. Pour 1½ cups of water into the bowl of the Instant Pot. Put a trivet or shallow steamer basket in the pot. Lay the chicken breasts in a single layer on the trivet. Secure the lid and seal the vent.

3. Select Pressure Cook or Manual and cook on high pressure for 6 minutes, then allow the pressure to naturally release for 5 minutes.

4. Quick release the remaining pressure in the pot and remove the lid. Press Cancel.

5. To confirm doneness, use a meat thermometer to ensure an internal temperature of at least 165°F.

TIP: Mix up the flavor profile by adding your favorite seasonings in step 1, such as Italian seasoning, lemon pepper, garlic powder, onion powder, or chili powder.

PER SERVING: Calories: 280; Total fat: 6g; Sodium: 865mg: Carbohydrates: 0g; Sugars: 0g; Protein: 52g

Easy Chicken Fajitas

SERVES 4 TO 6
PREP TIME: 10 minutes
PRESSURE BUILD: 5 to
10 minutes

COOK TIME: 11 minutes,
Sauté/High Pressure
PRESSURE RELEASE:
5 minutes, Natural
then Quick

TOTAL TIME: 31 to 36 minutes

NUT-FREE, UNDER
AN HOUR

Traditionally, fajitas are little strips of meat sautéed with peppers and onions and served with tortillas. Serve these fajitas with a side of Cauliflower Rice (page 112) in place of rice and use lettuce wraps to replace tortillas. Add a dollop of fresh guacamole and some salsa for additional color, flavor, and flair.

2 tablespoons avocado
  oil, divided
1 red bell pepper, seeded
  and sliced
1 yellow bell pepper, seeded
  and sliced
1 medium yellow onion, sliced

2 pounds boneless, skinless
  chicken breasts, cut into
  ½-inch-thick strips
4 garlic cloves, minced
1 tablespoon chili powder
2 teaspoons ground cumin
1 teaspoon smoked paprika

1 teaspoon sea salt
½ teaspoon freshly ground
  black pepper
¼ teaspoon ground cayenne
  pepper (optional)
½ cup chicken broth
¼ cup lime juice

1. Select Sauté on the Instant Pot. Heat 1 tablespoon of oil until it shimmers.

2. Add the bell peppers and onion and sauté about 3 to 5 minutes, until they start to soften. Remove from the pot and set aside.

3. Heat the remaining 1 tablespoon of oil until it shimmers. Sauté the chicken until browned, about 4 minutes, working in batches if necessary.

4. Add the garlic, chili powder, cumin, paprika, salt, black pepper, and cayenne pepper (if using).

5. Pour in the broth and lime juice. Using a wooden spoon, scrape up any browned bits stuck to the bottom of the pot. Press Cancel. Secure the lid and seal the vent.

6. Select Pressure Cook or Manual and cook on high pressure for 2 minutes, then allow the pressure to naturally release for 5 minutes. Quick release the remaining pressure in the pot and remove the lid. Press Cancel.

7. Stir in the peppers and onions before serving.

PER SERVING: Calories: 357; Total fat: 14g; Sodium: 863mg; Carbohydrates: 8g; Sugars: 3g; Protein: 52g

Chicken Cacciatore

SERVES 4

PREP TIME: 5 minutes

PRESSURE BUILD: 10 to 20 minutes

COOK TIME: 11 minutes, High Pressure

PRESSURE RELEASE: Quick

TOTAL TIME: 26 to 36 minutes

NUT-FREE, UNDER AN HOUR

The word cacciatore means "hunter" in Italian. Dating back to the Renaissance period, cacciatore was likely made with rabbit and other small game animals that hunters would catch. In modern cuisine, chicken cacciatore is a family favorite made with the classic ingredients tomato, rosemary, and thyme. Serve this dish on a bed of your favorite vegetable noodles such as spaghetti squash (page 110) or zucchini noodles (see tip on page 74), or atop a mound of Mashed "No-tatoes" (page 113).

1 (14.5-ounce) can diced tomatoes

1 medium red bell pepper, diced

1 small yellow or white onion, diced

2 garlic cloves, minced

1 tablespoon chopped fresh rosemary or 1 teaspoon dried

1 tablespoon chopped fresh thyme or 1 teaspoon dried

1½ pounds boneless, skinless chicken breasts

1 teaspoon sea salt

¼ teaspoon black pepper

1 bay leaf

1. In the bowl of the Instant Pot, combine the diced tomatoes with their juices, bell pepper, onion, garlic, rosemary, thyme, and ½ cup of water.

2. Season the chicken on both sides with the salt and black pepper. Place the chicken and the bay leaf into the bowl of the Instant Pot and toss to coat.

3. Secure the lid and seal the vent. Select Pressure Cook or Manual and cook on high pressure for 11 minutes, then quick release the pressure in the pot and remove the lid. Remove and discard the bay leaf before serving.

TIP: If you prefer a thicker sauce, remove the chicken after step 3 and cook the sauce on Sauté mode until it cooks down to your liking.

PER SERVING: Calories: 240; Total fat: 5g; Sodium: 837mg: Carbohydrates: 10g; Sugars: 5g; Protein: 39g

Whole "Roasted" Chicken with Vegetables

SERVES 4 TO 6
PREP TIME: 10 minutes
PRESSURE BUILD: 10 to 20 minutes

COOK TIME: 38 minutes, Sauté/High Pressure
PRESSURE RELEASE: 20 to 40 minutes, Natural

TOTAL TIME: 1 hour, 18 minutes to 1 hour, 48 minutes

NUT-FREE, WORTH THE WAIT

This recipe will have your guests thinking you spent all day in the kitchen. Try adding in root veggies such as parsnips or sweet potatoes. To save space, stuff the chicken cavity with the vegetables.

2 tablespoons extra-virgin olive oil

1 (3½- to 4-pound) whole chicken

1 teaspoon sea salt

1 teaspoon freshly ground black pepper

1 yellow onion, chopped

4 garlic cloves, minced

4 celery stalks, cut into 1-inch pieces

1 cup chicken broth or water

2 cups baby carrots or 1-inch carrot pieces

1 tablespoon poultry seasoning or Italian seasoning

1. Select Sauté on the Instant Pot. Heat the oil until it shimmers.

2. Season the chicken with the salt and pepper. Brown the chicken on both sides, 3 to 4 minutes per side, and then remove to a plate.

3. Combine the onion, garlic, and celery in the bowl of the Instant Pot and sauté until soft, 3 to 5 minutes. Using a slotted spoon, remove the vegetables from the pot, leaving the juices. Press Cancel.

4. Place a trivet or steamer rack in the bowl and pour in the broth. Set the chicken on the trivet and spoon the sautéed vegetables and carrots around the chicken. Sprinkle the poultry seasoning over top.

5. Secure the lid and seal the vent. Select Pressure Cook or Manual and cook on high pressure for 25 minutes, then allow the pressure to naturally release. Open the vent and remove the lid.

6. Transfer the chicken to a serving platter, arrange the vegetables around it, and spoon the chicken juices over to serve.

PER SERVING: Calories: 489; Total fat: 28g; Sodium: 1,050mg; Carbohydrates: 16g; Sugars: 7g; Protein: 43g

Herbed Chicken with Olives

SERVES 4 TO 6
PREP TIME: 10 minutes, plus
2 hours to marinate
PRESSURE BUILD: 5 to
10 minutes

COOK TIME: 20 minutes,
Sauté/High Pressure
PRESSURE RELEASE:
5 minutes, Natural
then Quick

TOTAL TIME: 2 hours,
40 minutes to 2 hours,
45 minutes

NUT-FREE, WORTH THE WAIT

Olives and their oil have been used over the millennia as medicine and food. They contain a unique fat and antioxidant profile that sets them apart in the fruit kingdom and makes them a popular choice in the Paleo world. This recipe calls for Kalamata, but is just as delicious with olives of any size, color, or flavor.

Juice of 3 lemons
3 garlic cloves, minced
½ cup chopped fresh parsley
2 tablespoons chopped fresh
   rosemary
2 chopped fresh sage leaves

8 pieces bone-in chicken
   parts (3½- to 4-pounds)
2 tablespoons extra-virgin
   olive oil
½ cup dry white wine

½ cup chicken broth
½ cup black salt-cured olives
   (such as Kalamata), pitted
Thin lemon slices, for garnish
   (optional)

1. In a large zip-top plastic bag, combine the lemon juice, garlic, parsley, rosemary, and sage. Add the chicken and toss to coat. Marinate in the refrigerator for 2 hours.

2. Select Sauté on the Instant Pot and heat the oil until it shimmers. Remove the chicken from the marinade (reserve the marinade) and brown on all sides in batches as needed, about 4 minutes. Remove the chicken from the pot and set aside. Press Cancel.

3. In the bowl of the Instant Pot, combine the marinade, wine, and broth. Add the chicken.

4. Secure the lid and seal the vent. Select Pressure Cook or Manual and cook on high pressure for 12 minutes.

5. Allow the pressure to naturally release for 5 minutes, then quick release the remaining pressure in the pot. Open the vent and remove the lid.

6. Serve chicken garnished with olives and lemon slices (if using).

TIP: You can substitute additional chicken broth for the white wine. If you don't have fresh herbs, use half the amount of dried herbs instead.

PER SERVING: Calories: 859; Total fat: 55g; Sodium: 532mg: Carbohydrates: 6g; Sugars: 1g; Protein: 78g

Lemon Chicken

SERVES 4 TO 6
PREP TIME: 5 minutes, plus
3 hours to marinate
PRESSURE BUILD: 5 to
10 minutes

COOK TIME: 16 minutes,
Sauté/High Pressure
PRESSURE RELEASE: Quick

TOTAL TIME: 3 hours,
26 minutes to 3 hours,
31 minutes

NUT-FREE, WORTH THE WAIT

While marinating, lemon juice brightens and tenderizes the chicken in this recipe. Oregano accentuates the tart crispness of the lemon, making for a mouthwatering dish. This recipe uses chicken breasts cut into long strips to infuse the lemon flavor, but you can use whole breasts or thighs instead.

2 pounds boneless, skinless chicken breasts, cut into 1-inch strips
¼ cup, plus 2 tablespoons extra-virgin olive oil

¼ cup freshly squeezed lemon juice
1 tablespoon dried oregano
1 teaspoon sea salt

1 teaspoon freshly ground black pepper
½ cup chicken broth

1. Put the chicken in a large zip-top plastic bag. In a small bowl, whisk together ¼ cup of oil, the lemon juice, oregano, salt, and pepper. Pour the marinade over the chicken and toss to coat. Marinate in the refrigerator for at least 3 hours.

2. Select Sauté on the Instant Pot. Heat the remaining 2 tablespoons of oil until it shimmers. Remove the chicken from the marinade (reserve the marinade) and sauté on both sides in batches as needed, about 4 minutes. Press Cancel.

3. Add the marinade and broth to the pot.

4. Secure the lid and seal the vent. Select Pressure Cook or Manual and cook on high pressure for 8 minutes, then quick release the pressure in the pot and remove the lid. Serve chicken with the marinade sauce.

TIP: We love this dish served on a bed of steamed broccoli or with a side of Herbed Asparagus (page 105).

PER SERVING: Calories: 448; Total fat: 26g; Sodium: 801mg; Carbohydrates: 2g; Sugars: 1g; Protein: 50g

30-Minute Chile Chicken

SERVES 4 TO 6
PREP TIME: 5 minutes
PRESSURE BUILD: 10 to 20 minutes

COOK TIME: 15 minutes, High Pressure

PRESSURE RELEASE: Quick

TOTAL TIME: 30 to 40 minutes

NUT-FREE, UNDER AN HOUR

This one-pot meal uses prepared salsa, peppers, and green chiles to save you prep time in the kitchen. If you purchase prechopped onion and jarred chopped garlic, all you have to do is to pour the ingredients into the bowl of the Instant Pot and cook for a few minutes! The result is a surprisingly complex flavor profile that will delight the senses.

3 pounds bone-in, chicken drumsticks and/or thighs, skin removed

1 (15-ounce) jar salsa verde (green chile salsa)

1 (28-ounce) can fire-roasted tomatoes, drained

1 (7-ounce) can chopped green chiles, drained

1 yellow or white onion, chopped

4 garlic cloves, minced

1 tablespoon ground cumin

1 teaspoon sea salt

1 tablespoon chopped jalapeño (optional)

1. In the bowl of the Instant Pot, combine the chicken, salsa verde, tomatoes, green chiles, onion, garlic, cumin, salt, and jalapeño (if using). Stir to mix well.

2. Secure the lid and seal the vent. Select Pressure Cook or Manual and cook on high pressure for 15 minutes, then quick release the pressure in the pot and remove the lid.

3. Use tongs to transfer the chicken to a plate. When the chicken is cool enough to handle, remove and discard the bones. Shred the chicken with two forks or cut it into bite-size pieces. Return the chicken to the sauce and stir to coat before serving.

TIP: Salsa verde is a green salsa made with tomatillos, which look similar to green tomatoes but are tarter. If you can't find salsa verde, regular red salsa will work just as well.

PER SERVING: Calories: 652; Total fat: 21g; Sodium: 2,710mg: Carbohydrates: 25g; Sugars: 12g; Protein: 86g

Buffalo Chicken Wings

SERVES 4
PREP TIME: 5 minutes
PRESSURE BUILD: 10 to 20 minutes

COOK TIME: 10 minutes, High Pressure
PRESSURE RELEASE: 5 minutes, Natural then Quick

TOTAL TIME: 30 to 40 minutes

NUT-FREE, UNDER AN HOUR

Yes, the classic Frank's RedHot Sauce is Paleo, but you can use whatever Paleo-friendly hot sauce you like, such as Tabasco, Trader Joe's Habanero Sauce, sriracha, or Cholula. It's Paleo as long as it does not contain any added sugar, additives, or preservatives. Complete the classic wings experience and serve with homemade sweet potato fries, carrot and celery strips, and Paleo-friendly ranch dressing for dipping.

3 pounds chicken wing pieces, separated at joints

1 cup ghee, melted

1 cup hot sauce (such as Frank's RedHot Original Cayenne Pepper Sauce)

2 tablespoons apple cider vinegar

1. Place a trivet in the inner cooking pot and pour in 1½ cups of water. Pile the wings on top of the trivet.

2. Secure the lid and seal the vent. Select Pressure Cook or Manual and cook on high pressure for 10 minutes, then allow the pressure to naturally release for 5 minutes. Quick release the remaining pressure in the pot and remove the lid.

3. Meanwhile, make the sauce by mixing the melted ghee, hot sauce, and vinegar in a large bowl until well blended.

4. When the wings are cooked, use tongs to remove them to the sauce and toss to coat. Serve and enjoy!

TIP: Broiling the wings after coating them with the sauce makes them extra tasty. Line a rimmed baking sheet with foil and arrange the wings in a single layer. Broil for 5 minutes, then return to the bowl of sauce. Place the wings back on the baking sheet and broil for 5 more minutes until lightly browned. Coat the wings with any remaining sauce before serving.

PER SERVING: Calories: 1,216; Total fat: 105g; Sodium: 2,537mg: Carbohydrates: <1g; Sugars: 0g; Protein: 63g

Cashew Chicken

SERVES 4
PREP TIME: 5 minutes
PRESSURE BUILD: 10 to
20 minutes

COOK TIME: 15 minutes,
Sauté/High Pressure
PRESSURE RELEASE: Quick

TOTAL TIME: 30 to
40 minutes

UNDER AN HOUR

Cashew chicken is a Chinese-inspired dish featuring tender chunks of chicken marinated in a light garlic and soy sauce. Serve this flavorful Paleo rendition over low-carb Cauliflower Rice (page 112).

1 tablespoon sesame oil
½ cup coconut aminos
3 tablespoons
   sugar-free ketchup
2 tablespoons apple
   cider vinegar
3 tablespoons orange juice
6 garlic cloves, minced
1-inch piece fresh
   ginger, minced

½ teaspoon Chinese
   five-spice powder
½ teaspoon red pepper flakes
   (optional)
2 pounds chicken breasts,
   boneless, skinless, cut into
   bite-size pieces
2 tablespoons coconut
   flour, divided
¼ teaspoon sea salt

¼ teaspoon freshly ground
   black pepper
1 tablespoon avocado oil or
   coconut oil
¾ cup cashews
2 scallions, both white and
   green parts, chopped
   (optional)
4 teaspoons sesame seeds
   (optional)

1. In a medium bowl, combine the sesame oil, coconut aminos, ketchup, vinegar, orange juice, garlic, ginger, five-spice powder, and red pepper flakes (if using). Set sauce aside.

2. In another bowl, toss the chicken with 1 tablespoon of coconut flour, the salt, and black pepper.

3. Select Sauté on the Instant Pot. Heat the avocado oil until it shimmers. Add the chicken in batches as needed, and sear on both sides, about 3 minutes, until the pieces start to brown. Press Cancel.

4. Place all the chicken into the Instant Pot and stir in the sauce. Secure the lid and seal the vent. Select Pressure Cook or Manual and cook on high pressure for 10 minutes, then quick release the pressure in the pot and remove the lid. Press Cancel.

5. Meanwhile, mix the remaining 1 tablespoon of coconut flour with 3 tablespoons of water. Set aside.

6. Select Sauté and add the coconut flour slurry. Cook, stirring occasionally, until the sauce has thickened, about 2 minutes. Stir in the cashews. Press Cancel.

7. Serve topped with scallions (if using) and sesame seeds (if using).

TIP: Add more or less red pepper flakes to turn the heat up or down, or add a few tien tsin (dried red hot peppers).

PER SERVING: Calories: 518; Total fat: 24g; Sodium: 933mg: Carbohydrates: 19g; Sugars: 9g; Protein: 55g

Game-Day Chili

SERVES 6 TO 8
PREP TIME: 10 minutes
PRESSURE BUILD: 10 to
20 minutes

COOK TIME: 15 minutes,
Sauté/High Pressure
PRESSURE RELEASE:
10 minutes, Natural
then Quick

TOTAL TIME: 45 to 55 minutes

NUT-FREE, UNDER AN HOUR

Whether you're serving this meal to family or to a crowd, this chili is a warm and comforting bowl of happiness. If you have Bone Broth in an Instant on hand (page 40), this is the perfect recipe to use it in. We love this meal on game day because it feeds up to 8 people.

2 tablespoons avocado oil

2 pounds ground turkey

¾ teaspoon sea salt

2 medium sweet potatoes, cut into 1-inch cubes

1 medium red onion, diced

3 garlic cloves, minced

4 celery stalks, chopped

3 carrots, chopped

1 red bell pepper, seeded and chopped

1 (14.5-ounce) can diced tomatoes

3 cups chicken broth

1 tablespoon chili powder

2 teaspoons ground cumin

1. Select Sauté on the Instant Pot. Heat the oil until it shimmers.

2. Add the turkey and salt. Sauté for 5 minutes, using a wooden spoon to break up the meat and keep it from sticking to the pot. Press Cancel.

3. Add the sweet potatoes, onion, garlic, celery, carrots, bell pepper, tomatoes with their juices, broth, chili powder, and cumin.

4. Secure the lid and seal the vent. Select Pressure Cook or Manual and cook on high pressure for 10 minutes, then naturally release the pressure in the pot for 10 minutes. Quick release any remaining pressure and remove the lid. Serve and enjoy!

TIP: Ground chicken or beef can be substituted for turkey, and any variety of sweet potato or color of bell pepper will work splendidly.

PER SERVING: Calories: 419; Total fat: 24g; Sodium: 1,061mg: Carbohydrates: 23g; Sugars: 8g; Protein: 29g

Turkey Bolognese

SERVES 6
PREP TIME: 5 minutes
PRESSURE BUILD: 5 to
10 minutes

COOK TIME: 21 to 31 minutes,
Sauté/High Pressure
PRESSURE RELEASE:
10 minutes, Natural
then Quick

TOTAL TIME: 41 to 56 minutes

UNDER AN HOUR

Ragù alla bolognese is a meat-based sauce developed in the mid-19th century by an Italian cook who lived in Bologna, Italy. The dish is typically slow-simmered to allow flavors to develop. The Instant Pot speeds up this process so you get all the wonderful Bolognese flavor in much less time. Try serving it with zoodles (see tip on page 74).

2 tablespoons extra-virgin
   olive oil
1 medium yellow
   onion, chopped
2 garlic cloves, minced
2 carrots, peeled and diced
   (about 1 cup)

2 tablespoons tomato paste
½ cup red wine
2 pounds ground turkey
1 teaspoon sea salt
½ teaspoon freshly ground
   black pepper

1 (28-ounce) can crushed
   tomatoes
½ cup unsweetened almond
   or coconut milk
1 teaspoon dried oregano

1. Select Sauté on the Instant Pot. Heat the oil until it shimmers.

2. Add the onion, garlic, carrots, and tomato paste and cook for 2 to 3 minutes, or until fragrant.

3. Pour the wine into the bowl of the Instant Pot. Using a wooden spoon, scrape up any browned bits stuck to the bottom.

4. Add the turkey, salt, and pepper. Use the wooden spoon to break the meat apart as it cooks, 5 to 8 minutes. Press Cancel.

5. Stir in the crushed tomatoes with their juices, milk, and oregano. Secure the lid and seal the vent. Select Pressure Cook or Manual and cook on high pressure for 10 minutes, then allow the pressure to naturally release for 10 minutes. Quick release any remaining pressure in the pot and remove the lid.

6. If you want to thicken the sauce, select Sauté and simmer, uncovered, for about 10 minutes. Stir and serve.

PER SERVING: Calories: 400; Total fat: 24g; Sodium: 768mg; Carbohydrates: 16g; Sugars: 9g; Protein: 29g

Duck with Mushrooms and Pearl Onions

SERVES 4

PREP TIME: 5 minutes

PRESSURE BUILD: 5 to 10 minutes

COOK TIME: 30 minutes, Sauté/High Pressure

PRESSURE RELEASE: 20 to 40 minutes, Natural

TOTAL TIME: 1 hour to 1 hour, 25 minutes

NUT-FREE

Duck is a very flavorful, nutrient-dense poultry that is often overlooked because it is thought to have a high fat content. The meat itself isn't fatty, but duck does have a layer of fat under the skin that is easily rendered off in your Instant Pot during the sauté stage.

2 tablespoons extra-virgin olive oil

4 duck legs

½ teaspoon sea salt

¼ teaspoon freshly ground black pepper

8 ounces pearl onions or white onion, chopped

8 ounces sliced mushrooms

4 garlic cloves, smashed

½ cup red wine

1 cup chicken broth

1. Select Sauté on the Instant Pot. Heat the oil until it shimmers.

2. Dry the duck well and season with salt and pepper. Place the duck, skin-side down, in the bowl of the Instant Pot and cook about 5 minutes, or until browned, in batches as needed. Set aside.

3. Carefully discard all but 2 tablespoons of the fat and oil in the pot (see Tip). Add the onions and sauté until softened, about 2 minutes. Add the mushrooms and garlic. Sauté, stirring, for 2 minutes more.

4. Add the wine and scrape up any browned bits off the bottom of the pot, cooking for 1 minute. Add the broth and duck. Press Cancel.

5. Secure the lid and seal the vent. Select Pressure Cook or Manual and cook on high pressure for 20 minutes, then allow the pressure to naturally release. Open the vent at the top and remove the lid.

6. Serve the duck with the onions, mushrooms, and cooking liquid spooned over top.

TIP: Instead of discarding it, you can save the rendered duck fat. It makes for a wonderful medium-heat cooking fat that is perfect for sautés. Feel free to substitute Bone Broth in an Instant (page 40) or water for the red wine.

PER SERVING: Calories: 398; Total fat: 20g; Sodium: 668mg; Carbohydrates: 9g; Sugars: 4g; Protein: 39g

CHAPTER 6

Seafood Mains

Steamed Fish and Veggies 66

15-Minute Mediterranean Halibut 67

Coconut Fish Curry 68

Almond Cod 69

Poached Salmon with Dill Sauce 70

Salmon and Vegetables en Papillote 71

Cilantro-Coconut Shrimp and Broccoli 72

Seafood Gumbo 73

Clams Steamed in Lemon-Garlic Broth 74

< Steamed Mussels with White Wine Sauce 75

Steamed Fish and Veggies

SERVES 4
PREP TIME: 10 minutes
PRESSURE BUILD: 5 to 10 minutes

COOK TIME: 8 minutes, Sauté/Low Pressure
PRESSURE RELEASE: Quick

TOTAL TIME: 23 to 28 minutes
NUT-FREE, UNDER 30 MINUTES

This visually striking dish features red tomatoes and green veggies against a background of flaky white fish. Saffron is a bright yellow-orange spice that comes from a flower and is the priciest spice in the world! Saffron adds an earthly floral flavor to dishes, but this recipe is just as delicious without it.

1 tablespoon ghee
1 small white onion, sliced
3 garlic cloves, minced
15 cherry tomatoes, halved
1 cup chopped zucchini
1 cup snow peas

4 small white fish fillets (about 1½ pounds total)
¼ cup chicken broth
1 lemon, cut into ¼-inch rounds

3 thyme sprigs or ½ teaspoon dried thyme
½ teaspoon sea salt
¼ teaspoon freshly ground black pepper
Pinch saffron (optional)

1. Select Sauté on the Instant Pot. Heat the ghee until melted.

2. Add the onion and cook for about 2 minutes, or until softened. Add the garlic and sauté for 1 minute more.

3. Add the tomatoes, zucchini, and snow peas to the pot. Add the fish on top, along with the broth, lemon, thyme, salt, pepper, and saffron (if using). Press Cancel.

4. Secure the lid and seal the vent. Select Pressure Cook or Manual and cook on low pressure for 5 minutes, then quick release the pressure in the pot and remove the lid.

5. Serve fish topped with the vegetables and sauce.

TIP: If you enjoy mild fish, cod is a great choice for this recipe. You can also use other varieties such as pollock, halibut, rockfish, or sea bass. If using frozen fish, add 2 minutes to the pressure cook time in step 4.

PER SERVING: Calories: 202; Total fat: 5g; Sodium: 514mg: Carbohydrates: 9g; Sugars: 5g; Protein: 32g

15-Minute Mediterranean Halibut

SERVES 2 TO 4
PREP TIME: 5 minutes
PRESSURE BUILD: 5 to 10 minutes

COOK TIME: 3 minutes, High Pressure
PRESSURE RELEASE: Quick

TOTAL TIME: 13 to 18 minutes

NUT-FREE, UNDER 30 MINUTES

The Paleo-friendly staples of Mediterranean cuisine generally include olives and olive oil, fruit and vegetables, nuts and seeds, fish and seafood, and herbs and spices. This Instant Pot dish takes the flavors of Greece and Italy and turns them into a glorious meal in under 15 minutes. Serve this dish with a side of lightly sautéed broccolini or a fresh green salad drizzled with olive oil and lemon juice.

1 (14.5-ounce) can diced tomatoes
½ cup pitted Kalamata olives

1 tablespoon freshly squeezed lemon juice
1 tablespoon capers
1 teaspoon dried oregano

4 (4-ounce) halibut fillets
½ teaspoon sea salt
½ teaspoon freshly ground black pepper

1. In the bowl of the Instant Pot, combine the diced tomatoes with their juices, olives, lemon juice, capers, and oregano.

2. Lay the halibut fillets on top of the tomato mixture and season with the salt and pepper.

3. Secure the lid and seal the vent. Select Pressure Cook or Manual and cook on high pressure for 3 minutes, then quick release the pressure in the pot and remove the lid. Serve.

TIP: If using canned tomatoes, it is best to opt for a BPA-free can. BPA is an industrial chemical known to be an endocrine (hormone) disrupter. You can replace the canned, diced tomatoes with 2 cups of fresh diced tomatoes instead.

PER SERVING: Calories: 360; Total fat: 13g; Sodium: 1,839mg; Carbohydrates: 13g; Sugars: 6g; Protein: 49g

Coconut Fish Curry

SERVES 4

PREP TIME: 5 minutes

PRESSURE BUILD: 5 to
10 minutes

COOK TIME: 6 minutes,
Sauté/High Pressure

PRESSURE RELEASE: 10 to
20 minutes, Natural

TOTAL TIME: 26 to 41 minutes

UNDER AN HOUR

In this dish, curry powder infuses coconut milk with smoky, slightly spicy flavor. There is no "one" recipe for curry powder, but the base ingredients almost always include turmeric, coriander, cumin, and chile peppers. Fresh ginger adds a surprising layer of flavor that is sweet yet peppery, while garlic and onion provide a familiar earthy warmth.

2 tablespoons coconut oil

1 large onion, sliced

3 garlic cloves, minced

1 tablespoon grated
fresh ginger

3 tablespoons curry powder

1½ pounds white fish fillets
(such as snapper, halibut,
or sole), cut into
1-inch pieces

1 teaspoon sea salt

1 (14-ounce) can full-fat
coconut milk

Juice of ½ lemon

1. Select Sauté on the Instant Pot. Heat the oil until it shimmers.

2. Add the onion and sauté until it begins to soften, 1 to 2 minutes. Add the garlic, ginger, and curry powder and sauté for another minute. Press Cancel.

3. Place the fish on top of the onion mixture and season with the salt. Pour the coconut milk and lemon juice over top.

4. Secure the lid and seal the vent. Select Pressure Cook or Manual and cook on high pressure for 3 minutes, then allow the pressure to naturally release. Open the vent at the top and remove the lid.

5. Serve in bowls and enjoy immediately.

TIP: To make your own curry powder from scratch, mix together equal parts ground turmeric, cumin, coriander, fenugreek seeds, ginger, mustard, cardamom, black pepper, cinnamon, and chile powder. Store in a sealed glass container for up to 1 year.

PER SERVING: Calories: 423; Total fat: 27g; Sodium: 731mg: Carbohydrates: 13g; Sugars: 6g; Protein: 36g

Almond Cod

SERVES 2 TO 4
PREP TIME: 5 minutes
PRESSURE BUILD: 5 to 10 minutes

COOK TIME: 6 minutes, Sauté/High Pressure
PRESSURE RELEASE: Quick

TOTAL TIME: 16 to 21 minutes

UNDER 30 MINUTES

This pot-in-pot recipe takes cod to the next level with an aromatic herb mixture that resembles chimichurri, an Argentinian sauce made with olive oil, garlic, parsley, oregano, and red wine vinegar. Our recipe creates an herb paste that's punctuated by crunchy toasted almonds. Fresh herbs are loaded with disease-fighting antioxidants, and almonds provide fiber, beneficial phytochemicals, and plenty of healthy monounsaturated fatty acids.

1 tablespoon extra-virgin olive oil

4 tablespoons sliced almonds, divided

3 garlic cloves, halved

½ cup fresh parsley leaves

1 teaspoon dried oregano

½ teaspoon paprika

¼ teaspoon sea salt

¼ teaspoon freshly ground black pepper

1 pound cod fillets

1 cup chicken broth

1. Select Sauté on the Instant Pot. Heat the oil until it shimmers.

2. Add 2 tablespoons of almonds and sauté, stirring frequently, until lightly browned, 1 to 2 minutes. Remove and set aside to drain on paper towels. Press Cancel.

3. In a food processor, pulse the garlic, parsley, oregano, paprika, salt, pepper, and remaining 2 tablespoons of almonds until a paste forms.

4. Slather the mixture on the cod fillets. Layer the fillets in a heatproof bowl that fits inside the pot. Cover the bowl with aluminum foil.

5. Place a trivet or steamer rack in the Instant Pot and pour in the chicken broth. Place the foil-covered bowl on the trivet. Secure the lid and seal the vent. Cook on high pressure for 4 minutes, then quick release the pressure in the pot and remove the lid.

6. Remove the foil from the bowl and place the fish on serving plates. Garnish with the browned almonds to serve.

PER SERVING: Calories: 347; Total fat: 16g; Sodium: 971mg; Carbohydrates: 6g; Sugars: 1g; Protein: 45g

Poached Salmon with Dill Sauce

SERVES 4
PREP TIME: 5 minutes
PRESSURE BUILD: 5 to 10 minutes

COOK TIME: 9 minutes, High Pressure/Sauté
PRESSURE RELEASE: Quick

TOTAL TIME: 19 to 24 minutes

UNDER 30 MINUTES

Salmon is king of the sea when it comes to nutrition. Loaded with protein and anti-inflammatory omega-3 fatty acids, regular consumption promotes heart and brain health. Opt for wild-caught salmon when possible and aim to consume fatty seafood at least 2 to 3 times per week.

1 (20-ounce) center-cut salmon fillet
½ teaspoon sea salt
¼ teaspoon freshly ground black pepper
4 teaspoons dried dill, divided

Zest of 1 small lemon (about 2 teaspoons)
Juice of 1 small lemon (about 2 tablespoons)
½ cup dry white wine
½ cup chicken broth

1 bay leaf
4 scallions, both white and green parts, chopped
1 tablespoon tapioca flour or arrowroot flour
2 tablespoons coconut cream

1. Season the salmon with the salt, pepper, and 1 teaspoon of dill.

2. In the bowl of the Instant Pot, combine the lemon zest, lemon juice, wine, broth, and bay leaf. Place a trivet or steamer basket in the bowl and then place the salmon on top. Sprinkle with the scallions.

3. Secure the lid and seal the vent. Select Pressure Cook or Manual and cook on high pressure for 6 minutes, then quick release the pressure in the pot and remove the lid. Press Cancel.

4. Remove the salmon to a serving platter and tent it with a piece of aluminum foil.

5. Remove the trivet and select Sauté. Bring the liquid to a boil and add the remaining 3 teaspoons of dill and the tapioca flour. Cook for 2 to 3 minutes, whisking constantly, until the sauce thickens. Remove the bay leaf. Stir in the coconut cream.

6. Pour the sauce over the salmon to serve.

TIP: Coconut cream separates to the top in cans of full-fat coconut milk. Refrigerate your can overnight to facilitate the cream's separation from the coconut water.

PER SERVING: Calories: 220; Total fat: 7g; Sodium: 629mg: Carbohydrates: 5g; Sugars: 4g; Protein: 28g

Salmon and Vegetables en Papillote

SERVES 2
PREP TIME: 10 minutes
PRESSURE BUILD: 5 to 10 minutes

COOK TIME: 6 minutes, High Pressure
PRESSURE RELEASE: Quick

TOTAL TIME: 21 to 26 minutes

NUT-FREE, UNDER 30 MINUTES

This quick-and-easy recipe uses parchment paper or foil as a pouch to lock in moisture and flavor. For a unique serving presentation, unwrap the salmon pouch at the dinner table.

1 teaspoon ghee, at room temperature
1 (12-ounce) salmon fillet
½ teaspoon sea salt
¼ teaspoon freshly ground black pepper

2 tablespoons finely minced scallions, green parts only
1 small tomato, seeded and diced (about ½ cup)
⅓ cup sugar snap peas, trimmed

¼ cup sliced mushrooms
2 or 3 whole fresh flat-leaf parsley leaves (optional)

1. Take a piece of unbleached parchment paper or foil, 15 by 20 inches or larger, and smear the ghee in the center, spreading it out so the salmon will fit on the greased portion. Place the salmon on the parchment and season with the salt and pepper.

2. Sprinkle the scallions and tomato over the fish. Sprinkle the snap peas and mushrooms around the salmon and top with the parsley leaves (if using).

3. Lift the longer sides of the parchment or foil, bringing the edges together above the salmon like a tent. Fold them over several times, leaving some air space over the fish and vegetables. Then crimp the short ends, sealing the pouch tightly.

4. Put 1½ cups of water in the Instant Pot and insert a trivet. Place the salmon pouch on top of the trivet.

5. Secure the lid and seal the vent. Select Pressure Cook or Manual and cook on high pressure for 6 minutes, then quick release the pressure in the pot and remove the lid.

6. Remove the salmon pouch to a serving platter, open, and serve.

TIP: You can remove the skin from the fish before cooking, but it is a rich source of healthy omega-3 fatty acids. We recommend that you make it a habit to eat the whole fish, from tip to tail!

PER SERVING: Calories: 213; Total fat: 7g; Sodium: 811mg: Carbohydrates: 2g; Sugars: 4g; Protein: 34g

Cilantro-Coconut Shrimp and Broccoli

SERVES 2 TO 4
PREP TIME: 10 minutes
PRESSURE BUILD: 5 to 10 minutes

COOK TIME: 8 minutes, Low Pressure
PRESSURE RELEASE: Quick

TOTAL TIME: 23 to 28 minutes

UNDER 30 MINUTES

This Thai-inspired meal takes a classic pairing of shrimp and broccoli to new gustatory heights. Cilantro is the superstar herb of Thai cuisine and a main ingredient in this dish. If you don't like cilantro, you can substitute it with Thai basil.

1 (14-ounce) can full-fat coconut milk

2 cups loosely packed fresh cilantro

1 jalapeño pepper, seeded and cut into chunks

1 scallion, green part only, cut into chunks

2 garlic cloves

1½ teaspoons sea salt

12 ounces broccoli florets

16 ounces peeled large shrimp, fresh

1. In a blender, blend the coconut milk, cilantro, jalapeño pepper, scallion, garlic, and salt until smooth.

2. Select Sauté on the Instant Pot. Pour the sauce into the pot and add ¼ cup of water. Bring the mixture to a simmer. Press Cancel.

3. Place a steamer basket in the pot and add the broccoli. Layer the shrimp over the broccoli.

4. Secure the lid and seal the vent. Cook on low pressure for 8 minutes, then quick release the pressure in the pot and remove the lid.

5. Gently remove the broccoli and shrimp from the steamer basket into the sauce and stir to coat. Serve.

TIP: For a spicy version, garnish with red pepper flakes or a few squirts of sriracha, a Thai hot sauce.

PER SERVING: Calories: 558; Total fat: 37g; Sodium: 3,103mg; Carbohydrates: 22g; Sugars: 10g; Protein: 37g

Seafood Gumbo

SERVES 6
PREP TIME: 10 minutes
PRESSURE BUILD: 10 to 20 minutes

COOK TIME: 8 minutes, Sauté/High Pressure
PRESSURE RELEASE: 5 minutes, Natural then Quick

TOTAL TIME: 33 to 43 minutes

NUT-FREE, UNDER AN HOUR

Seafood gumbo is a cherished dish in Louisiana cooking. This Paleo-friendly version does not use a roux, so if you prefer a thicker gumbo, add 8 to 16 ounces of fresh or frozen okra. The soluble fiber in this fruit (yes, it's a fruit!) is a natural thickener.

2 tablespoons extra-virgin olive oil

1 yellow onion, diced

2 garlic cloves, minced

2 celery stalks, diced

2 cups chicken broth

1 (14-ounce) can diced fire-roasted tomatoes

1 pound halibut fillets, patted dry and cut into 2-inch cubes

1 pound medium tail-on shrimp, peeled and deveined

½ teaspoon ground cayenne pepper

1 teaspoon dried oregano

1 teaspoon dried thyme

2 teaspoons paprika

½ teaspoon sea salt

½ teaspoon freshly ground black pepper

1. Select Sauté on the Instant Pot. Heat the oil until it shimmers.

2. Add the onion, garlic, and celery and sauté for 3 minutes, stirring occasionally. Press Cancel.

3. Pour the broth and diced tomatoes with their juices into the pot. Using a wooden spoon, scrape up any browned bits stuck to the bottom. Add the halibut, shrimp, cayenne pepper, oregano, thyme, paprika, salt, and black pepper. Stir to combine.

4. Secure the lid and seal the vent. Select Pressure Cook or Manual and cook on high pressure for 5 minutes, then allow the pressure to naturally release for 5 minutes. Quick release the remaining pressure in the pot and remove the lid.

5. Stir and serve.

TIP: Another authentic way to thicken your gumbo without using a roux is to add filé, the dried and ground leaves of the sassafras tree. Simply add ½ to 1 teaspoon to each bowl of gumbo.

PER SERVING: Calories: 225; Total fat: 6g; Sodium: 1,123mg: Carbohydrates: 7g; Sugars: 3g; Protein: 30g

Clams Steamed in Lemon-Garlic Broth

SERVES 2 TO 4
PREP TIME: 5 minutes
PRESSURE BUILD: 5 to 10 minutes

COOK TIME: 4 to 6 minutes, Sauté/High Pressure
PRESSURE RELEASE: Quick

TOTAL TIME: 14 to 21 minutes

NUT-FREE, UNDER 30 MINUTES

Clams are perfect Paleo eats of the sea. As a source of many vitamins and minerals, clams are particularly rich in selenium, iron, riboflavin, and vitamin B_{12}. They are also a source of anti-inflammatory omega-3 fatty acids and high-quality protein. Your Instant Pot steams them up in just a few minutes for a simple and elegant meal.

4 tablespoons ghee, divided
4 garlic cloves, minced
1 cup dry white wine

4 pounds littleneck clams, thoroughly scrubbed

2 tablespoons freshly squeezed lemon juice, plus more as needed
¼ cup chopped fresh parsley

1. Select Sauté on the Instant Pot.

2. Melt 2 tablespoons of ghee and sauté the garlic for 1 to 2 minutes until fragrant. Pour in the white wine. Add the clams and stir to coat with the liquid. Press Cancel.

3. Secure the lid and seal the vent. Select Pressure Cook or Manual and cook on high pressure for 2 minutes, then quick release the pressure in the pot and remove the lid. Press Cancel. The clams should be opened; if not, replace, *but don't lock*, the lid. Press Sauté and cook for 1 to 2 minutes more. Discard any clams that still have not opened.

4. Stir in the remaining 2 tablespoons of ghee along with the lemon juice and parsley. When the ghee has melted, pour the clams with their sauce into a large bowl and enjoy.

TIP: Serve this dish over "zoodles" or spiralized zucchini noodles. Zoodles can be purchased or made with a vegetable peeler or spiralizer. Season zoodles with salt and pepper and sauté in oil for 1 or 2 minutes until softened.

PER SERVING: Calories: 1,116; Total fat: 34g; Sodium: 5,464mg: Carbohydrates: 39g; Sugars: 2g; Protein: 134g

Steamed Mussels with White Wine Sauce

SERVES 2 TO 4
PREP TIME: 10 minutes
PRESSURE BUILD: 5 to 10 minutes

COOK TIME: 5 to 7 minutes, Sauté/Low Pressure
PRESSURE RELEASE: Quick

TOTAL TIME: 20 to 27 minutes

NUT-FREE, UNDER 30 MINUTES

Like their mollusk cousin the clam, mussels are nutritional powerhouses. They're chock-full of vitamins and minerals, with a 3-ounce serving providing more than 100 percent of the recommended daily amount of selenium and vitamin B_{12}.

2 pounds fresh mussels

1 tablespoon extra-virgin olive oil

3 large shallots or 1 small red onion, minced

3 garlic cloves, thinly sliced

½ cup dry white wine

½ cup chicken broth

Pinch red pepper flakes (optional)

3 tablespoons lemon juice

Chopped fresh parsley or dill, for garnish

1. Thoroughly clean the mussels using a dry brush and cold water. Remove the beards and discard any mussels that are not tightly shut.

2. Select Sauté on the Instant Pot. Heat the oil until it shimmers.

3. Add the shallots and garlic and sauté for about 2 minutes until fragrant.

4. Add the mussels, wine, broth, and red pepper flakes (if using) and stir to coat.

5. Secure the lid and seal the vent. Select Pressure Cook or Manual and cook on low pressure for 3 minutes, then quick release the pressure in the pot and remove the lid. The mussels should be opened; if not, replace, *but don't lock*, the lid. Press Sauté and cook for 1 to 2 minutes more. Discard any mussels that still have not opened.

6. Pour the mussels with their sauce into a large bowl. Serve topped with the lemon juice and fresh parsley.

TIP: Serve this dish over "swoodles" or spiralized sweet potato noodles. They can be purchased or made with a vegetable peeler or spiralizer. Sauté swoodles in oil for 2 or 3 minutes until softened.

PER SERVING: Calories: 600; Total fat: 17g; Sodium: 1,547mg: Carbohydrates: 42g; Sugars: 11g; Protein: 58g

CHAPTER 7

Beef Mains

Roast Beef and Roots 78

Barbacoa Beef 79

Instant Meatballs 80

Sweet and Sour Meatloaf 81

Hearty Beef Chili 82

Moroccan-Inspired Beef 83

Thai-Inspired Red Curry Beef 84

Beef and Broccoli 85

Corned Beef and Cabbage 86

Pot Roast with Winter Vegetables 87

Beef Stroganoff 88

< Korean-Inspired Short Ribs 89

Roast Beef and Roots

SERVES 6
PREP TIME: 10 minutes
PRESSURE BUILD: 10 to
20 minutes

COOK TIME: 1 hour,
10 minutes, Sauté/High
Pressure
PRESSURE RELEASE:
10 minutes, Natural
then Quick

TOTAL TIME: 1 hour,
40 minutes to 1 hour,
50 minutes

NUT-FREE, WORTH THE WAIT

This hearty dish creates a roast so tender that it cuts like butter and melts in your mouth. The surprising combination of chili powder and ground cinnamon is a common spice pairing in the Midwest, where chili is often eaten with a cinnamon roll on the side. In this meal, sweet potatoes and carrots provide a much healthier, Paleo-friendly option.

1 tablespoon extra-virgin
olive oil, tallow, or lard
1 tablespoon chili powder
1 teaspoon ground cinnamon
1 teaspoon sea salt

½ teaspoon freshly ground
black pepper
1 (3-pound) boneless
beef roast
2 large sweet potatoes, cut
into 2-inch chunks

4 large carrots, quartered,
cut into 2-inch chunks
1 large onion, chopped
1 cup beef broth

1. Select Sauté on the Instant Pot. Heat the oil until it shimmers.

2. In a small bowl, mix the chili powder, cinnamon, salt, and pepper. Set aside.

3. Sear the roast on all sides until browned, about 10 minutes. Press Cancel.

4. Rub the spice mixture over the top and sides of the roast and arrange the sweet potatoes, carrots, and onion around it. Pour the beef broth over top.

5. Secure the lid and seal the vent. Select Pressure Cook or Manual and cook on high
pressure for 1 hour, then allow the pressure to release naturally for 10 minutes. Quick
release any remaining pressure in the pot and remove the lid.

6. Using two forks, remove the roast from the Instant Pot and serve with the vegetables.

TIP: To make gravy, in a small bowl, whisk 2 teaspoons of tapioca flour or arrowroot flour and ¼ cup of beef broth until dissolved. Select Sauté and bring the remaining broth in the pot to a boil. Whisk in the tapioca mixture and cook for 2 minutes, or until the broth has thickened.

PER SERVING: Calories: 534; Total fat: 30g; Sodium: 829mg; Carbohydrates: 22g; Sugars: 6g; Protein: 46g

Barbacoa Beef

SERVES 4 TO 6
PREP TIME: 10 minutes
PRESSURE BUILD: 5 to
10 minutes

COOK TIME: 35 minutes,
Sauté/High Pressure
PRESSURE RELEASE:
10 minutes, Natural
then Quick

TOTAL TIME: 1 hour to 1 hour,
5 minutes

NUT-FREE, WORTH THE WAIT

Barbacoa is authentic to the cuisine of Mexico. It's usually a preparation of beef that is slow cooked in broth to tender perfection with an array of chiles and spices. You can use whatever cut of beef you prefer, but chuck roast is affordable with lots of flavor. Trim off any visible fat before cooking.

2 tablespoons extra-virgin
olive oil, tallow, or lard
2 pounds beef chuck roast,
cut into 2-inch cubes
1 yellow onion, diced
4 garlic cloves, minced

1 tablespoon dried oregano
2 teaspoons ground cumin
1 teaspoon chili powder
1 teaspoon sea salt
½ teaspoon freshly ground
black pepper

1 cup beef broth
Juice of 2 limes
1 (4-ounce) can diced
green chiles

1. Select Sauté on the Instant Pot. Heat the oil until it shimmers.

2. Add the beef, onion, garlic, oregano, cumin, chili powder, salt, and pepper. Sauté for 5 minutes, stirring occasionally. Press Cancel.

3. Pour the broth, lime juice, and chiles over the meat in the pot. Using a wooden spoon, scrape up any browned bits stuck to the bottom.

4. Secure the lid and seal the vent. Select Pressure Cook or Manual and cook on high pressure for 30 minutes, then allow the pressure to naturally release for 10 minutes. Quick release the remaining pressure in the pot and remove the lid.

5. Stir the mixture. If you want to shred the beef, use two forks to pull apart each piece. Serve on salad greens or in lettuce leaf tacos.

TIP: To turn up the heat of your barbacoa, add up to ¼ teaspoon of ground cayenne pepper with the other spices in step 2.

PER SERVING: Calories: 640; Total fat: 47g; Sodium: 1,033mg: Carbohydrates: 8g; Sugars: 3g; Protein: 47g

Instant Meatballs

SERVES 4 TO 6

PREP TIME: 10 minutes

PRESSURE BUILD: 5 to
10 minutes

COOK TIME: 12 minutes,
Sauté/High Pressure

PRESSURE RELEASE:
5 minutes, Natural
then Quick

TOTAL TIME: 32 to 37 minutes

UNDER AN HOUR

This recipe makes tender, flavorful meatballs and a delicious homemade tomato sauce that's healthier and tastier than store-bought sauce. For more nutrition, add ¼ cup of grated liver to the meatballs.

1½ pounds ground beef,
  turkey, chicken, or lamb

1 large egg

½ cup almond flour or meal

1½ teaspoon sea salt, divided

1 teaspoon onion powder

½ teaspoon garlic powder

1 tablespoon avocado oil

1 (28-ounce) can crushed
  tomatoes

1 (14-ounce) can diced
  tomatoes

1 medium onion, chopped

3 garlic cloves, minced

1 tablespoon Italian
  seasoning

¼ teaspoon freshly ground
  black pepper

1 (6-ounce) can tomato paste

1. In a large mixing bowl, combine the ground beef, egg, almond meal, 1 teaspoon of salt, the onion powder, and garlic powder. Mix well. Shape the meat mixture into 2-inch meatballs. Set aside.

2. Select Sauté on the Instant Pot. Heat the oil until it shimmers. Add the meatballs and brown on all sides, about 5 minutes, working in batches as needed. Press Cancel.

3. In a large bowl, stir together the crushed and diced tomatoes with their juices, onion, garlic, Italian seasoning, ½ teaspoon of salt, the pepper, and tomato paste. Place the meatballs in the Instant Pot, pour in the sauce, and gently toss to coat.

4. Secure the lid and seal the vent. Select Pressure Cook or Manual and cook on high pressure for 7 minutes, then allow the pressure to naturally release for 5 minutes. Quick release the remaining pressure in the pot and remove the lid. Serve.

TIP: Serve this dish over zoodles (see tip on page 74). Make this recipe nut-free by substituting ½ cup of ground pork rinds in place of the almond flour.

PER SERVING: Calories: 686; Total fat: 37g; Sodium: 1,599mg: Carbohydrates: 36g; Sugars: 19g; Protein: 55g

Sweet and Sour Meatloaf

SERVES 4 TO 6
PREP TIME: 15 minutes
PRESSURE BUILD: 10 to 20 minutes

COOK TIME: 30 minutes, High Pressure
PRESSURE RELEASE: 10 minutes, Natural then Quick

TOTAL TIME: 1 hour, 5 minutes to 1 hour, 15 minutes

NUT-FREE, WORTH THE WAIT

Touches of sweet honey and sour vinegar put a zesty spin on this quintessential American classic. Raw honey and apple cider vinegar contain nutrients, antioxidants, and enzymes that promote disease prevention.

3 tablespoons sugar-free ketchup
1 tablespoon honey
1 tablespoon apple cider vinegar
2 dried bay leaves

1 pound ground beef
¼ cup finely chopped onions
½ green bell pepper, chopped
½ cup ground pork rinds
1 large egg

1 tablespoon Italian seasoning
½ teaspoon sea salt
½ teaspoon freshly ground black pepper

1. Place a trivet in the pot and pour in 1½ cups of water. On top of the trivet, place a 12-inch square of aluminum foil with the edges folded upward along the curves of the pot.

2. In a small bowl, stir together the ketchup, honey, and vinegar. Add the bay leaves. Set aside.

3. In a large bowl, combine the beef, onions, bell pepper, pork rinds, egg, Italian seasoning, salt, and black pepper. Mix with your hands to combine well, then shape the meatloaf mixture into a 6- to 7-inch loaf that will fit in the Instant Pot. Place it on the foil. Pour the ketchup mixture over the top.

4. Secure the lid and seal the vent. Select Pressure Cook or Manual and cook on high pressure for 30 minutes, then allow the pressure to naturally release for 10 minutes. Quick release the remaining pressure in the pot and remove the lid.

5. Remove the bay leaves. Carefully lift the foil from the Instant Pot to remove the meatloaf. Serve and enjoy!

PER SERVING: Calories: 343; Total fat: 19g; Sodium: 585mg; Carbohydrates: 8g; Sugars: 6g; Protein: 34g

Hearty Beef Chili

SERVES 6 TO 8
PREP TIME: 5 minutes
PRESSURE BUILD: 10 to 20 minutes

COOK TIME: 15 minutes, Sauté/High Pressure
PRESSURE RELEASE: 10 minutes, Natural then Quick

TOTAL TIME: 40 to 50 minutes

NUT-FREE, UNDER AN HOUR

While chili is thought of as a cold-weather staple, it is an ideal meal for any time of year. Instead of beans, you can add seasonal veggies: chunks of pumpkin or butternut squash in the fall and winter, and zucchini or sturdy leafy greens such as kale in the spring and summer.

2 tablespoons avocado oil
1 large yellow onion, diced
4 garlic cloves, minced
2 pounds lean ground beef
2 tablespoons chili powder
2 teaspoons ground cumin

1 teaspoon sea salt
1 teaspoon freshly ground black pepper
1 teaspoon smoked paprika (optional)
2 cups beef broth

1 large sweet potato, cut into 1-inch chunks
1 (28-ounce) can fire-roasted crushed tomatoes
1 cup sliced black olives

1. Select Sauté on the Instant Pot. Heat the oil until it shimmers.

2. Sauté the onion, garlic, ground beef, chili powder, cumin, salt, pepper, and smoked paprika (if using) for 3 to 5 minutes, until the beef starts to brown. Press Cancel.

3. Pour in the broth. Using a wooden spoon, scrape up any browned bits stuck to the bottom of the pot. Add the sweet potatoes, tomatoes with their juices, and olives. Stir to combine.

4. Secure the lid and seal the vent. Select Pressure Cook or Manual and cook on high pressure for 10 minutes, then allow the pressure to naturally release for 10 minutes. Quick release any remaining pressure in the pot and remove the lid. Serve.

TIP: Top with sliced jalapeño, fresh cilantro, shredded carrots, radish slices, or chopped chives for a colorful finish.

PER SERVING: Calories: 461; Total fat: 21g; Sodium: 1,302mg; Carbohydrates: 23g; Sugars: 9g; Protein: 46g

Moroccan-Inspired Beef

SERVES 4 TO 6
PREP TIME: 10 minutes
PRESSURE BUILD: 10 to 20 minutes

COOK TIME: 54 minutes, Sauté/High Pressure
PRESSURE RELEASE: 20 to 40 minutes, Natural

TOTAL TIME: 1 hour, 34 minutes to 2 hours, 4 minutes

NUT-FREE, WORTH THE WAIT

The flavors of Morocco shine brightly in this Paleo take on a traditional beef tagine. A tagine is a North African stew slow cooked in clay or ceramic cookware. The Instant Pot adds speed to traditional tagine recipes without losing any original tastes or textures. Aromatic spices infuse bold layers of flavor into this distinctive recipe.

1 tablespoon ghee or extra virgin olive oil
1½ pounds beef chuck roast, cut into 2-inch pieces
1 large onion, diced
3 garlic cloves, minced
1 teaspoon ground cumin

1 teaspoon ground ginger
1 teaspoon ground turmeric
1 teaspoon sea salt
½ teaspoon ground coriander
½ teaspoon ground cinnamon
½ teaspoon freshly ground black pepper

1½ cups beef broth
½ cup black or green olives, pitted
¼ cup chopped fresh parsley and/or cilantro
Pinch saffron (optional)
Juice of ½ lemon

1. Select Sauté on the Instant Pot. Heat the ghee until it melts.

2. Add the meat, in batches if necessary, and brown on all sides, 6 to 8 minutes. Add the onion, garlic, cumin, ginger, turmeric, salt, coriander, cinnamon, and pepper to the meat and sauté, stirring constantly, for 1 minute. Stir in the broth, olives, parsley, and saffron (if using). Press Cancel.

3. Secure the lid and seal the vent. Select Pressure Cook or Manual and cook on high pressure for 45 minutes. Allow the pressure to naturally release. Open the vent and remove the lid. Stir in the lemon juice and serve.

TIP: To make this in a slow cooker, combine all the ingredients, cover, and cook on high heat for 6 hours, or on low heat for 8 hours.

PER SERVING: Calories: 489; Total fat: 35g; Sodium: 1,156mg: Carbohydrates: 7g; Sugars: 2g; Protein: 35g

Thai-Inspired Red Curry Beef

SERVES 4 TO 6

PREP TIME: 10 minutes

PRESSURE BUILD: 10 to 20 minutes

COOK TIME: 13 minutes, High Pressure/Sauté

PRESSURE RELEASE: 10 minutes, Natural then Quick

TOTAL TIME: 43 to 53 minutes

UNDER AN HOUR

As a staple of Thai cuisine, red curry paste is the foundation of many popular curry dishes. Mixed with coconut milk, it creates a distinctive smoky, spicy, and creamy base for meat and veggies. We love the flavor of flank steak, but you can use any type of meat or poultry you like.

- 2 (14-ounce) cans full-fat coconut milk
- 3 to 4 ounces Thai red curry paste (6 to 8 tablespoons)
- 2 pounds flank steak or flat-iron steak, cut into ¼-inch-thick slices against the grain
- 1 red onion, sliced
- 1 medium zucchini, cut into ¼-inch rounds then cut into half-moons
- 1 medium red bell pepper, seeded and cut into 1-inch pieces
- 1 pint cherry tomatoes, halved
- ½ teaspoon sea salt
- ¼ cup coarsely chopped fresh basil or cilantro
- 1 tablespoon honey (optional)
- 1 teaspoon freshly squeezed lime juice (optional)
- ½ teaspoon fish sauce (optional)
- 2 tablespoons coconut aminos (optional)

1. Pour the coconut milk into the bowl of the Instant Pot. Add the curry paste and whisk to combine. Add the steak and onion.

2. Secure the lid and seal the vent. Select Pressure Cook or Manual and cook on high pressure for 7 minutes, then allow the pressure to release naturally for 10 minutes. Quick release any remaining pressure in the pot and remove the lid. Press Cancel.

3. Select Sauté. Add the zucchini, bell pepper, and tomatoes to the meat in the pot and bring to a simmer. Cook, stirring occasionally, for 5 to 6 minutes, or until the vegetables are tender. Stir in the salt and basil. If using, stir in the honey, lime juice, fish sauce, and coconut aminos.

TIP: Serve this dish over Cauliflower Rice (page 112) or swoodles (see tip on page 75). Save time by chopping the veggies while the meat is pressure cooking.

PER SERVING: Calories: 800; Total fat: 55g; Sodium: 890mg: Carbohydrates: 21g; Sugars: 13g; Protein: 53g

Beef and Broccoli

SERVES 4 TO 6
PREP TIME: 10 minutes
PRESSURE BUILD: 5 to 10 minutes

COOK TIME: 21 minutes, Sauté/High Pressure
PRESSURE RELEASE: Quick

TOTAL TIME: 36 to 41 minutes

UNDER AN HOUR

This version of the Chinese classic cooks up quickly in your Instant Pot. The beef is tender and the broccoli is crisp and bright. Serve this dish over Cauliflower Rice (page 112).

2 tablespoons coconut oil, divided

1½ pounds flank steak, skirt steak, or tri-tip, cut into ¼-inch-thick slices against the grain

1 yellow onion, diced

1½ tablespoons garlic, minced

½ teaspoon red pepper flakes

½ teaspoon sea salt

½ teaspoon freshly ground black pepper

1 cup beef broth

⅓ cup coconut aminos

1 tablespoon tapioca flour

1 pound broccoli florets (2 to 3 broccoli crowns)

1 tablespoon toasted sesame oil

2 scallions, both white and green parts, chopped (optional)

1. Select Sauté on the Instant Pot. Heat 1 tablespoon of coconut oil until it shimmers.

2. Sauté the beef in batches until browned, about 5 minutes. Transfer to a plate and set aside.

3. Add the remaining 1 tablespoon of coconut oil to the pot and sauté the onion, garlic, red pepper flakes, salt, and black pepper for about 1 minute until fragrant, stirring constantly.

4. Add the broth, coconut aminos, and browned beef to the Instant Pot. Stir to combine. Press Cancel.

5. Secure the lid and seal the vent. Select Pressure Cook or Manual and cook on high pressure for 10 minutes. Quick release the pressure in the pot and remove the lid. Press Cancel.

6. Mix the tapioca flour with 1 tablespoon of water to form a slurry. Select Sauté and add the tapioca slurry and broccoli to the beef in the pot. Stir frequently for 3 to 5 minutes, until the broccoli is tender and the sauce has thickened. Press Cancel. Stir in the sesame oil.

7. Garnish with scallions (if using) and serve.

PER SERVING: Calories: 475; Total fat: 25g; Sodium: 1,009mg: Carbohydrates: 15g; Sugars: 7g; Protein: 40g

Corned Beef and Cabbage

SERVES 6 TO 8
PREP TIME: 5 minutes
PRESSURE BUILD: 10 to 20 minutes

COOK TIME: 1 hour, 48 minutes, High Pressure
PRESSURE RELEASE: 20 to 40 minutes, Natural and Quick

TOTAL TIME: 2 hours, 23 minutes to 2 hours, 52 minutes

NUT-FREE, WORTH THE WAIT

When Irish immigrants settled in New York, they brought a favored dish of bacon and potatoes with them. At the time, corned beef and cabbage were cheaper and easier to procure than bacon and potatoes. Hence, the iconic pairing was born.

1 (3- to 4-pound) corned beef brisket
1 bay leaf
4 or 5 whole peppercorns
1 teaspoon dried thyme

3 or 4 whole allspice berries or ⅛ teaspoon ground allspice
2 cups beef broth

4 large carrots, cut into 1-inch pieces
1 small head green cabbage, root end trimmed, cut into 8 wedges

1. In the bowl of the Instant Pot, combine the corned beef, bay leaf, peppercorns, thyme, and allspice. Pour in the broth and 2 cups of water.

2. Secure the lid and seal the vent. Cook on high pressure for 1 hour and 45 minutes, then allow the pressure to naturally release. Open the vent and remove the lid. Press Cancel.

3. Transfer the corned beef to a cutting board and tent with aluminum foil, reserving the broth in the pot.

4. Add the carrots and cabbage to the Instant Pot.

5. Secure the lid and seal the vent. Cook on high pressure for 3 minutes, then quick release the pressure in the pot. Remove the lid.

6. Meanwhile, slice the corned beef against the grain into thick slices.

7. Remove the bay leaf and discard. Serve the corned beef with vegetables and cooking liquid over top.

TIP: If your brisket comes with a Paleo-friendly spice packet (with no added sugar or preservatives), use it instead of the bay leaf, peppercorns, thyme, and allspice for an easier preparation.

PER SERVING: Calories: 505; Total fat: 34g; Sodium: 3,112mg: Carbohydrates: 12g; Sugars: 6g; Protein: 36g

Pot Roast with Winter Vegetables

SERVES 4 TO 6
PREP TIME: 5 minutes
PRESSURE BUILD: 10 to 20 minutes

COOK TIME: 1 hour, 5 minutes, Sauté/High Pressure
PRESSURE RELEASE: 10 minutes, Natural then Quick

TOTAL TIME: 1 hour, 30 minutes to 1 hour, 40 minutes

NUT-FREE, WORTH THE WAIT

American pot roast was adapted from the French *bœuf à la mode,* or "beef in style." In the classic preparation, a tough cut of meat is seared in hot oil to lock in the juices, then slow-simmered to tenderize and develop flavor. Your Instant Pot cooks pot roast to perfection in a quarter of the time that slow cooking would.

1 (2½-pound) beef chuck (shoulder) roast

1 teaspoon sea salt

1 teaspoon freshly ground black pepper

1 tablespoon extra-virgin olive oil

2 cups beef broth

2 tablespoons tomato paste

1 large onion, chopped

2 cups parsnips, cut into 2-inch lengths

2 cups carrots, cut into 2-inch lengths

3 celery stalks, cut into 2-inch lengths

4 to 6 garlic cloves, chopped (optional)

1 tablespoon Italian seasoning (optional)

1. Season the roast on all sides with the salt and pepper.

2. Select Sauté on the Instant Pot. Heat the oil until it shimmers. Add the meat and brown on both sides, about 5 minutes. Remove to a plate and set aside. Press Cancel.

3. Add the broth and tomato paste, scraping any browned bits stuck to the bottom of the pot with a wooden spoon. Return the roast to the liquid in the pot and cover with the onion, parsnips, carrots, celery, garlic (if using), and Italian seasoning (if using).

4. Secure the lid and seal the vent. Select Pressure Cook or Manual and cook on high pressure for 1 hour, then allow the pressure to naturally release for 10 minutes. Quick release any remaining pressure in the pot and remove the lid.

5. Slice the roast against the grain into thick pieces. Serve with the vegetables and sauce poured over top.

TIP: You can swap in Jerusalem artichokes (sunchokes) to replace the parsnips.

PER SERVING: Calories: 513; Total fat: 18g; Sodium: 1,325mg: Carbohydrates: 25g; Sugars: 10g; Protein: 64g

Beef Stroganoff

SERVES 4 TO 6
PREP TIME: 5 minutes
PRESSURE BUILD: 10 to 20 minutes

COOK TIME: 23 minutes, Sauté/High Pressure
PRESSURE RELEASE: 20 to 40 minutes, Natural

TOTAL TIME: 58 minutes to 1 hour, 28 minutes

WORTH THE WAIT

Beef Stroganoff is a popular dish originating from Russia. The Instant Pot makes this Paleo version a cinch to prepare so you can enjoy it any night of the week.

3 tablespoons extra-virgin olive oil
¾ cup tapioca flour or arrowroot flour
2 teaspoons sea salt
1 teaspoon freshly ground black pepper

1 teaspoon onion powder
1 teaspoon dried thyme
1 teaspoon dried rosemary
½ teaspoon paprika
1 (2-pound) sirloin tip roast, cut into cubes

1 onion, thinly sliced
4 garlic cloves, minced
1½ cups beef broth
¼ cup dry red wine
1 cup coconut cream

1. Select Sauté on the Instant Pot. Heat the oil until it shimmers.

2. In a large bowl, combine the tapioca flour, salt, pepper, onion powder, thyme, rosemary, and paprika. Toss the meat cubes in the seasoned flour.

3. Add the meat to the pot and sauté until browned, 2 to 3 minutes. Cook the meat in batches, if necessary. Press Cancel.

4. Add the onion, garlic, broth, and wine to the Instant Pot, scraping any browned bits stuck to the bottom of the pot.

5. Secure the lid and seal the vent. Select Pressure Cook or Manual and cook on high pressure for 20 minutes, then allow the pressure to naturally release. Open the vent and remove the lid.

6. Stir in the coconut cream. Serve the stroganoff over the vegetable noodles of your choice (see Tip).

TIP: Replace traditional egg noodles with zoodles (see tip on page 74), swoodles (see tip on page 75), or spaghetti squash (page 110).

PER SERVING: Calories: 570; Total fat: 27g; Sodium: 2,030mg: Carbohydrates: 27g; Sugars: 2g; Protein: 48g

Korean-Inspired Short Ribs

SERVES 4

PREP TIME: 10 minutes, plus 20 minutes to marinate

PRESSURE BUILD: 10 to 20 minutes

COOK TIME: 40 minutes, High Pressure

PRESSURE RELEASE: 15 minutes, Natural then Quick

TOTAL TIME: 1 hour, 35 minutes to 1 hour, 45 minutes

WORTH THE WAIT

This Korean-inspired short rib recipe is marinated to perfection and is fall-off-the-bone tender. Conventional short ribs are widely available, but if you can find Korean-style cross-cut, bone-in beef short ribs (flanken style), use them instead.

4 pounds bone-in, beef short ribs

1 teaspoon sea salt

1 large onion, cut into chunks

1 large Asian or Bosc pear, peeled and cut into chunks

8 garlic cloves

2 tablespoons minced fresh ginger

½ cup dry sherry, white wine, or chicken broth

⅔ cup coconut aminos

2 tablespoons sriracha or chile-garlic paste

¼ cup honey

4 scallions, green part only, thinly sliced

1. Sprinkle the ribs on all sides with the salt. Place in a resealable plastic bag and let sit while you prepare the marinade.

2. For the marinade, place the onion and pear chunks in a blender or food processor. Add the garlic, ginger, sherry, coconut aminos, sriracha, and honey. Blend until the mixture is fairly smooth.

3. Pour the marinade over the ribs, manipulating the bag to fully coat. Let them sit at room temperature for 20 to 60 minutes.

4. Pour the ribs and marinade into the Instant Pot. Secure the lid and seal the vent. Select Pressure Cook or Manual and cook on high pressure for 40 minutes, then allow the pressure to naturally release for 15 minutes. Quick release any remaining pressure in the pot and remove the lid.

5. Using tongs, remove the ribs to a platter or shallow bowl. If you like, simmer the sauce for a few minutes to thicken.

6. To serve, spoon some of the sauce over the ribs and sprinkle with the scallions.

PER SERVING: Calories: 1,108; Total fat: 57g; Sodium: 1,656mg: Carbohydrates: 45g; Sugars: 33g; Protein: 86g

CHAPTER 8

Pork Mains

Pork Carnitas 92

Spanish-Inspired Pork 93

Easy Hawaiian-Style Pork 94

Pork Roast with Apples 95

Blackberry-Glazed Pork Chops 96

Mac 'n' Cheese 'n' Ham 97

Honey Mustard Pork Tenderloin 98

Holiday Honey Ham 99

Baby Back Instant Pot Ribs 100

< Sausage-Stuffed Peppers 101

Pork Carnitas

SERVES 4 TO 6
PREP TIME: 5 minutes
PRESSURE BUILD: 5 to
10 minutes

COOK TIME: 1 hour,
6 minutes, Sauté/High
Pressure
PRESSURE RELEASE:
10 minutes, Natural
then Quick

TOTAL TIME: 1 hour,
26 minutes to 1 hour,
31 minutes

NUT-FREE, WORTH THE WAIT

Resembling pulled pork, carnitas originated in the mountains of Michoacán, Mexico. Pork is cooked in oil or lard until tender and juicy, and served on tortillas made from non-Paleo grains like corn and wheat. You can purchase Paleo-friendly tortillas made from almond, coconut, tapioca, or cassava flour, or make your own. Large leafy greens also work well as a tortilla stand-in.

2 tablespoons extra-virgin olive oil or lard

2 pounds boneless pork roast, cut into 2 or 3 pieces to fit inside the pot

½ cup chicken broth

½ cup orange juice

1 tablespoon dried oregano

2 teaspoons ground cumin

1 teaspoon chili powder

1 teaspoon garlic powder

1 teaspoon sea salt

½ teaspoon freshly ground black pepper

Juice of 2 limes

1. Select Sauté on the Instant Pot. Heat the oil until it shimmers.

2. Add the pork and brown for 3 minutes per side. Press Cancel.

3. Pour in the broth and orange juice. Using a wooden spoon, scrape up any browned bits stuck to the bottom of the pot. Add the oregano, cumin, chili powder, garlic powder, salt, and pepper. Stir to combine.

4. Secure the lid and seal the vent. Select Pressure Cook or Manual and cook on high pressure for 1 hour, then allow the pressure to naturally release for 10 minutes. Quick release any remaining pressure in the pot and remove the lid.

5. Stir in the lime juice. Using two forks, shred the pork. Serve and enjoy!

TIP: Pork shoulder, butt roast, or shoulder blade roast work best for this recipe.

PER SERVING: Calories: 471; Total fat: 25g; Sodium: 815mg: Carbohydrates: 7g; Sugars: 3g; Protein: 49g

Spanish-Inspired Pork

SERVES 6 TO 8
PREP TIME: 5 minutes
PRESSURE BUILD: 10 to 20 minutes

COOK TIME: 43 minutes, Sauté/High Pressure
PRESSURE RELEASE: 20 to 40 minutes, Natural

TOTAL TIME: 1 hour, 18 minutes to 1 hour, 48 minutes

NUT-FREE, WORTH THE WAIT

Pork butt comes from the shoulder of the pig, although it is not the same as pork shoulder. Also known as "Boston butt," pork butt is located higher on the foreleg, while pork shoulder is farther down. These cuts of meat are often slow cooked for hours to make them more tender. The Instant Pot significantly speeds up this process. In only an hour, you'll have a flavorful and versatile main course that pairs perfectly with your veggie of choice.

3 tablespoons extra-virgin olive oil or lard

3 pounds pork butt, cut into 1-inch cubes

3 large carrots, cut into 1-inch pieces

2 parsnips, cut into 1-inch pieces

1 medium onion, chopped

6 garlic cloves, diced

2 cups chicken broth

1 cup dry red wine

⅓ cup lemon juice

1 tablespoon paprika

2 teaspoons sea salt

¼ cup chopped fresh parsley

1. Select Sauté on the Instant Pot. Heat the oil until it shimmers.

2. Sauté the meat, in batches as needed, 2 to 3 minutes, until browned. Press Cancel.

3. Add the carrots, parsnips, onion, garlic, broth, wine, lemon juice, paprika, and salt to the meat in the pot. Stir to combine.

4. Secure the lid and seal the vent. Cook on high pressure for 40 minutes, then allow the pressure to naturally release. Open the vent and remove the lid.

5. Garnish with parsley and serve.

TIP: Pork shoulder can also be used for this recipe. This dish is delicious served with Mashed "No-tatoes" (page 113).

PER SERVING: Calories: 536; Total fat: 31g; Sodium: 1,621mg: Carbohydrates: 15g; Sugars: 5g; Protein: 38g

Easy Hawaiian-Style Pork

SERVES 6 TO 8
PREP TIME: 5 minutes
PRESSURE BUILD: 10 to 20 minutes

COOK TIME: 1 hour, 30 minutes, High Pressure
PRESSURE RELEASE: 20 to 40 minutes, Natural

TOTAL TIME: 2 hours, 5 minutes to 2 hours, 30 minutes

NUT-FREE, WORTH THE WAIT

If you've ever been to a traditional Hawaiian luau, you may have had kālua pork. Cooked in an underground oven called an imu for half a day or more, the result is pork that is deliciously smoky and salty. Your Instant Pot brings you the flavors of Hawaii in a fraction of the time. Serve with Maple-Balsamic Parsnips (page 106) or Lemon-Steamed Artichokes (page 104) for a complete meal.

1½ tablespoons Hawaiian red salt or sea salt
1 tablespoon dried oregano
1 teaspoon freshly ground black pepper

1 (5-pound) bone-in pork roast
1 (20-ounce) can pineapple chunks

1 yellow or white onion, quartered
6 garlic cloves, smashed

1. In a small bowl, mix together the salt, oregano, and pepper. Set aside.

2. Cut the pork roast into 3 equal pieces. Rub each piece with the salt mixture. Place in the bottom of the Instant Pot in a single layer.

3. Add the pineapple with its juice, onion, and garlic to the pot.

4. Secure the lid and seal the vent. Select Pressure Cook or Manual and cook on high pressure for 1½ hours, then allow the pressure to naturally release. Open the vent and remove the lid.

5. Cut or shred the pork and serve.

TIP: Canned pineapple chunks are featured in this recipe, but you can use tidbits, slices, crushed, or fresh pineapple if you prefer. If you use fresh pineapple, add 1 cup of water with the rest of the ingredients in step 3.

PER SERVING: Calories: 539; Total fat: 20g; Sodium: 2,388mg; Carbohydrates: 18g; Sugars: 14g; Protein: 65g

Pork Roast with Apples

SERVES 6

PREP TIME: 5 minutes

PRESSURE BUILD: 10 to 20 minutes

COOK TIME: 1 hour, 11 minutes, Sauté/High Pressure

PRESSURE RELEASE: 15 to 30 minutes, Natural

TOTAL TIME: 1 hour, 41 minutes to 2 hours, 6 minutes

NUT-FREE, WORTH THE WAIT

Apples are the perfect companion to pork. We recommend choosing a firm variety of apple for this recipe, such as Granny Smith, Honeycrisp, Pink Lady, or Gala. This dish calls for apple juice. While we do not recommend drinking fruit juice due to the high sugar content, cooking with it is just fine.

1 teaspoon caraway seed, crushed

1 teaspoon ground cinnamon

1 teaspoon ground mustard

1 teaspoon dried thyme

1 teaspoon sea salt

½ teaspoon freshly ground black pepper

1 (3- to 3½-pound) pork shoulder roast, trimmed

2 tablespoons avocado oil

1 onion, cut into wedges

1 cup apple juice

3 apples, cored and cut into wedges

1. In a small bowl, combine the caraway, cinnamon, mustard, thyme, salt, and pepper. Rub the mixture all over the outside of the pork.

2. Select Sauté and heat the oil until it shimmers. Brown the meat on all sides, 6 to 8 minutes. Press Cancel.

3. Add the onion and apple juice to the meat in the pot.

4. Secure the lid and seal the vent. Cook for 1 hour on high pressure, then allow the pressure to naturally release. Press Cancel.

5. Remove the roast to a platter and tent with aluminum foil.

6. Select Sauté and add the apple wedges to the juices in the pot. Simmer for 3 minutes. Remove the foil, pour the apples and juices over the roast, and serve immediately.

TIP: Caraway seeds are the dried fruit of the caraway plant. They have a distinctive, aromatic, mild licorice flavor. They taste similar to anise seed, which can be substituted into this recipe instead.

PER SERVING: Calories: 502; Total fat: 29g; Sodium: 899mg; Carbohydrates: 24g; Sugars: 14g; Protein: 35g

Blackberry-Glazed Pork Chops

SERVES 2

PREP TIME: 5 minutes

PRESSURE BUILD: 5 to 10 minutes

COOK TIME: 10 minutes, Sauté/High Pressure

PRESSURE RELEASE: 5 minutes, Natural then Quick

TOTAL TIME: 25 to 30 minutes

NUT-FREE, UNDER 30 MINUTES

A "berry" fancy glaze elevates these ordinary pork chops to the next culinary level. The sweetness of blackberries and honey collides with zesty Dijon to deliver lively flavor to your plate in less than 30 minutes. Taste-bud nirvana awaits!

2 tablespoons avocado oil

2 boneless pork loin chops, about 1-inch thick

½ teaspoon sea salt

¼ teaspoon freshly ground black pepper

¼ cup blackberry jam

1 tablespoon Dijon mustard

1 tablespoon honey

1. Select Sauté on the Instant Pot. Heat the oil until it shimmers.

2. Season the chops with the salt and pepper, then brown them, about 3 minutes per side. Remove and set aside.

3. Pour 1½ cups of water into the pot, scraping up any browned bits from the bottom and sides. Press Cancel.

4. Place a trivet in the pot and set the chops on the trivet.

5. In a small bowl, whisk together the jam, mustard, and honey. Pile the mixture on top of each pork chop.

6. Secure the lid and seal the vent. Select Pressure Cook or Manual and cook on high pressure for 4 minutes, then allow the pressure to naturally release for 5 minutes. Quick release the remaining pressure in the pot and remove the lid. Serve and enjoy!

TIP: This recipe calls for blackberry jam, but any flavor of jelly, fruit spread, or even preserves will work.

PER SERVING: Calories: 420; Total fat: 20g; Sodium: 840mg; Carbohydrates: 35g; Sugars: 33g; Protein: 23g

Mac 'n' Cheese 'n' Ham

SERVES 4
PREP TIME: 5 minutes
PRESSURE BUILD: 10 to 20 minutes

COOK TIME: 1 minute, Low Pressure
PRESSURE RELEASE: Quick

TOTAL TIME: 16 to 26 minutes
UNDER 30 MINUTES

This Paleo version of macaroni and cheese swaps in healthy cauliflower for the noodles and dairy-free nutritional yeast sauce for the cheese. We use cubed ham steak, but you can sub in chopped hot dogs for a quick kid-friendly meal. Not all ham steaks and hot dogs are Paleo, so be sure to select a brand that is all natural, uncured, and free from hormones and antibiotics.

½ cup full-fat coconut milk
¾ cup nutritional yeast, divided
1 tablespoon Dijon mustard
½ teaspoon sea salt
½ teaspoon freshly ground black pepper

½ teaspoon onion powder
½ teaspoon garlic powder
½ teaspoon ground turmeric (optional)
½ pound ham steak, cut into ½-inch cubes

1 head cauliflower, cut into florets (about 6 cups)
2 tablespoons ghee, melted
4 scallions, both white and green parts, diced

1. In a small bowl, stir together the coconut milk, 6 tablespoons of nutritional yeast, the mustard, salt, pepper, onion powder, garlic powder, and turmeric (if using).

2. Add the ham cubes and cauliflower florets to the Instant Pot and pour the coconut milk mixture over the top. Stir in the ghee.

3. Secure the lid and seal the vent. Select Pressure Cook or Manual and cook on low pressure for 1 minute, then quick release the pressure in the pot and remove the lid. Press Cancel.

4. Stir in the remaining 6 tablespoons of nutritional yeast. Garnish with the scallions and serve hot.

TIP: Transform this into a vegan recipe by omitting the ham and swapping in coconut oil for the ghee. You can also use unsweetened almond or another nut milk instead of coconut milk.

PER SERVING: Calories: 318; Total fat: 16g; Sodium: 1,164mg: Carbohydrates: 20g; Sugars: 5g; Protein: 28g

Honey Mustard Pork Tenderloin

SERVES 6

PREP TIME: 5 minutes

PRESSURE BUILD: 5 to
10 minutes

COOK TIME: 17 minutes,
Sauté/High Pressure

PRESSURE RELEASE:
10 minutes, Natural
then Quick

TOTAL TIME: 37 to 42 minutes

NUT-FREE, UNDER AN HOUR

Not to be confused with pork loin, pork tenderloin is a boneless, lean, and tender cut of meat from the backbone muscle. Because it's so lean, it can easily dry out when overcooked. Fret not; your Instant Pot will lock in all the flavor and moisture in this simple-to-prepare dish.

2 tablespoons extra-virgin
olive oil or lard

2 tablespoons arrowroot flour
or tapioca flour

2 pounds pork tenderloin

1½ teaspoons sea
salt, divided

1 cup chicken broth

3 garlic cloves, minced

2 tablespoons Dijon mustard

¼ cup honey

¼ teaspoon freshly ground
black pepper

1. Select Sauté on the Instant Pot. Heat the oil until it shimmers.

2. In a small bowl, make a slurry by whisking together the arrowroot flour and ¼ cup of water. Set aside.

3. Season the pork with 1 teaspoon of salt. Add the pork to the pot and brown it for 2 minutes per side. Transfer the pork to a plate. Press Cancel.

4. Pour the broth into the pot. Using a wooden spoon, scrape up any browned bits stuck to the bottom of the pot. Add the garlic, mustard, honey, remaining ½ teaspoon of salt, and the pepper. Stir to combine.

5. Place a trivet inside the pot and place the pork on the trivet. Secure the lid and seal the vent. Select Pressure Cook or Manual and cook on high pressure for 8 minutes, then allow the pressure to naturally release for 10 minutes. Quick release any remaining pressure in the pot and remove the lid. Transfer the pork to a cutting board. Press Cancel.

6. Select Sauté and whisk the arrowroot slurry into the liquid. Simmer, uncovered, for 3 to 5 minutes, or until the sauce starts to thicken.

7. Slice the pork and serve topped with the sauce.

PER SERVING: Calories: 276; Total fat: 10g; Sodium: 1,555mg; Carbohydrates: 17g; Sugars: 12g; Protein: 30g

Holiday Honey Ham

SERVES 6 TO 8

PREP TIME: 5 minutes

PRESSURE BUILD: 10 to 20 minutes

COOK TIME: 16 to 18 minutes, High Pressure

PRESSURE RELEASE: 15 minutes, Natural then Quick

TOTAL TIME: 46 to 58 minutes

UNDER AN HOUR

Most holiday hams are precooked but require about 15 minutes per pound to heat in the oven. The Instant Pot will knock hours off your cooking time and present a juicy, flavor-packed ham. If you have a larger ham, you can trim it to fit in your pot. Say goodbye to dry ham that's been cooking for hours and liberate your oven for other uses during the holidays!

½ cup coconut sugar

¼ cup honey

¼ cup orange juice

¼ teaspoon ground cinnamon

⅛ teaspoon ground cloves

⅛ teaspoon ground nutmeg

Zest of 1 orange (optional)

3 to 4 pounds boneless spiral-sliced ham

1. Place a trivet in the Instant Pot. Pour in 1½ cups of water.

2. In a medium bowl, make the glaze by whisking together the coconut sugar, honey, orange juice, cinnamon, cloves, nutmeg, and orange zest (if using).

3. Place the ham on a piece of foil large enough to completely wrap around the ham. Brush half the glaze over the top, being sure to get some between the ham slices. Seal the foil around the ham and place it on the trivet in the pot.

4. Secure the lid and seal the vent. Select Pressure Cook or Manual and cook on high pressure for 2 minutes per pound plus 10 additional minutes. Allow the pressure to naturally release for 15 minutes, then quick release the remaining pressure in the pot and remove the lid.

5. Brush the ham with the remaining glaze and serve.

TIP: Instead of honey, swap in maple syrup for a delicious maple-glazed ham. Serve with your favorite variety of mustard on the side.

....

PER SERVING: Calories: 401; Total fat: 13g; Sodium: 2,027mg: Carbohydrates: 32g; Sugars: 31g; Protein: 43g

Baby Back Instant Pot Ribs

SERVES 4 TO 6
PREP TIME: 5 minutes
PRESSURE BUILD: 10 to 20 minutes

COOK TIME: 30 minutes, High Pressure
PRESSURE RELEASE: 15 minutes, Natural then Quick

TOTAL TIME: 1 hour to 1 hour, 10 minutes

NUT-FREE, WORTH THE WAIT

Fall-off-the-bone tender, these savory pork ribs will elicit some serious finger-licking from your guests! When purchasing baby back ribs, search for ones that are uniform in thickness with even marbling. Serve with a side of Creamed Coconut Kale (page 107) or Herbed Asparagus (page 105) to complete the meal.

1 rack baby back pork ribs, with membrane removed
2 tablespoons paprika

1 tablespoon garlic powder
1 tablespoon onion powder
1 tablespoon chipotle powder

1½ teaspoons ground cumin
1 tablespoon sea salt
1 cup beef broth

1. Place the ribs on a clean cutting board. Set aside.

2. In a small bowl, combine the paprika, garlic powder, onion powder, chipotle powder, cumin, and salt. Rub the spice mix over the ribs, covering them completely.

3. Pour the beef broth into the Instant Pot, then place a trivet inside the pot. Place the ribs on the trivet, standing up on their short side and wrapping around the inside of the pot.

4. Secure the lid and seal the vent. Select Pressure Cook or Manual and cook on high pressure for 30 minutes, then allow the pressure to release naturally for 15 minutes. Quick release any remaining pressure in the pot and remove the lid. Serve and enjoy!

TIP: If you like sauce with your ribs, serve them with a Paleo-friendly barbecue sauce on the side. You can also brush the cooked ribs with barbecue sauce and place them on a baking sheet under the broiler for 5 minutes to brown.

PER SERVING: Calories: 496; Total fat: 33g; Sodium: 2,099mg: Carbohydrates: 7g; Sugars: 1g; Protein: 42g

Sausage-Stuffed Peppers

SERVES 4
PREP TIME: 10 minutes
PRESSURE BUILD: 10 to 20 minutes

COOK TIME: 18 minutes, Sauté/High Pressure
PRESSURE RELEASE: Quick

TOTAL TIME: 38 to 48 minutes

NUT-FREE, UNDER AN HOUR

Easy to make but elegant enough for dinner guests, these stuffed peppers are destined to join your regular rotation! You can use any color of bell pepper that you prefer. Enjoy as a stand-alone meal or serve with a fresh green salad on the side.

1 tablespoon avocado oil
1 pound ground pork
½ cup finely chopped onion
2 cups raw cauliflower rice
1 small tomato, chopped

1 teaspoon oregano
1 teaspoon paprika
1 teaspoon sea salt
½ teaspoon black pepper

¼ teaspoon ground cumin
4 medium bell peppers
1 tablespoon chopped fresh
  parsley (optional)

1. Select Sauté on the Instant Pot. Heat the oil until it shimmers.

2. Add the pork and onion and sauté for 5 minutes.

3. Add the cauliflower rice, tomato, oregano, paprika, salt, black pepper, cumin, and ½ cup of water. Sauté, stirring occasionally, until the mixture is warmed through and starts to thicken, about 5 minutes. Press Cancel.

4. Meanwhile, cut the tops off the bell peppers and remove the seeds.

5. Fill the bell peppers with equal portions of the pork mixture, mounding it up over the tops. Set aside.

6. Pour 1½ cups of water into the pot. Place a trivet on the bottom and place the stuffed peppers on the trivet.

7. Secure the lid and seal the vent. Select Pressure Cook or Manual and cook on high pressure for 8 minutes, then quick release the pressure in the pot and remove the lid. Remove the peppers and garnish with parsley (if using).

TIP: You can purchase premade cauliflower rice or make your own by grating cauliflower over a box grater or pulsing it in a food processor until you achieve a grain-like consistency.

PER SERVING: Calories: 341; Total fat: 22g; Sodium: 682mg: Carbohydrates: 14g; Sugars: 8g; Protein: 24g

CHAPTER 9

Vegetarian Mains and Sides

Lemon-Steamed Artichokes 104

Herbed Asparagus 105

Maple-Balsamic Parsnips 106

Creamed Coconut Kale 107

Cider-Braised Brussels Sprouts 108

"Baked" Sweet Potatoes 109

Spaghetti Squash Primavera 110

Beet Marinara Sauce 111

Cauliflower Rice 112

Mashed "No-tatoes" 113

Sesame Bok Choy 114

Gobi Masala 115

< Vegetable Korma 116

Lemon-Steamed Artichokes

SERVES 2

PREP TIME: 2 minutes

PRESSURE BUILD: 5 to 10 minutes

COOK TIME: 25 minutes, High Pressure

PRESSURE RELEASE: Quick

TOTAL TIME: 32 to 37 minutes

VEGAN, NUT-FREE, UNDER AN HOUR

The delicate meat of artichoke leaves and hearts infuses with lemon and garlic under pressure to yield pull-apart tenderness. These globes of nutritional goodness are high in fiber, vitamins, minerals, and disease-fighting antioxidants. Removing the stem helps them sit flat while trimming the top third and leaf tips (use a pair of scissors for the leaf tips) removes some of the inedible portions and provides a neat and polished appearance.

2 medium to large artichokes, tops and stems trimmed

1 lemon

½ teaspoon garlic salt

1. Pour 1½ cups of water into the Instant Pot and place a trivet or steamer rack in the bottom.

2. Arrange the artichokes standing up on the trivet, stem-side down.

3. Squeeze the juice from half of the lemon over each artichoke, then sprinkle with garlic salt, trying to get some of the seasoning under the leaves.

4. Secure the lid and seal the vent. Select Pressure Cook or Manual. Cook on high pressure for 25 minutes, then quick release the pressure in the pot and remove the lid.

5. Using tongs, remove the artichokes from the pot and serve.

TIP: Artichoke leaves are delicious served with mayonnaise or melted ghee. Paleo-friendly mayo is typically made from avocado or coconut oil and can be found in many supermarkets. Opt for grass-fed ghee when possible. If tolerated, grass-fed butter works as well.

PER SERVING: Calories: 86; Total fat: <1g; Sodium: 395mg; Carbohydrates: 20g; Sugars: 2g; Protein: 6g

Herbed Asparagus

SERVES 4 TO 6
PREP TIME: 2 minutes
PRESSURE BUILD: 5 to 10 minutes

COOK TIME: 1 minute, High Pressure
PRESSURE RELEASE: Quick

TOTAL TIME: 8 to 13 minutes

VEGAN, NUT-FREE, UNDER 30 MINUTES

Asparagus is a nutrient-packed veggie that's also nourishing for your intestinal microbiome—the population of microbes that flourishes in your gut. Due to the type of fiber it contains, called inulin, asparagus acts as a prebiotic and feeds beneficial bacteria. A healthy colony of intestinal bacteria aids in digestion and absorption, and promotes a healthy you!

1 pound asparagus spears, woody ends trimmed

1 tablespoon extra-virgin olive oil
½ teaspoon Italian seasoning

½ teaspoon sea salt
¼ teaspoon freshly ground black pepper

1. Pour 1½ cups of water into the Instant Pot and place a steamer basket or trivet in the bottom.

2. Arrange the asparagus in the basket and drizzle with the oil. Sprinkle with the Italian seasoning, salt, and pepper.

3. Secure the lid and seal the vent. Select Pressure Cook or Manual and cook on high pressure for 1 minute, then quick release the pressure in the pot and remove the lid.

4. Using tongs, remove the asparagus and serve.

TIP: Use any variety of spices you like in place of the Italian seasoning. Try herbes de Provence, lemon pepper, garlic powder, or ¼ teaspoon each of dried basil, rosemary, and thyme.

....

PER SERVING: Calories: 53; Total fat: 4g; Sodium: 295mg: Carbohydrates: 5g; Sugars: 2g; Protein: 3g

Maple-Balsamic Parsnips

SERVES 4

PREP TIME: 5 minutes

PRESSURE BUILD: 5 to 10 minutes

COOK TIME: 2 to 3 minutes, High Pressure

PRESSURE RELEASE: Quick

TOTAL TIME: 12 to 18 minutes

VEGAN, NUT-FREE, UNDER 30 MINUTES

Parsnips look like cream-colored carrots. They're a cool-season root veggie often relegated to winter soups and stews. When artfully steamed in your Instant Pot with touches of sweet balsamic vinegar and maple syrup and a sprinkle of earthy thyme, parsnips hold their own as a unique side dish with layers of flavor.

2 or 3 parsnips, peeled and cut into ½-inch pieces

2 garlic cloves, minced

½ cup applesauce

¼ cup maple syrup

2 tablespoons balsamic vinegar

2 tablespoons extra-virgin olive oil

½ teaspoon dried thyme

¼ teaspoon sea salt

1. In the bowl of your Instant Pot, combine the parsnips, garlic, applesauce, maple syrup, vinegar, oil, thyme, and salt.

2. Secure the lid and seal the vent. Select Pressure Cook or Manual and cook on high pressure for 2 minutes, then quick release the pressure in the pot and remove the lid.

3. If the parsnips are too firm for your liking, cook for another minute on high pressure.

TIP: If you aren't able to get parsnips, carrots are a great substitute in this recipe. Honey can be used in place of the maple syrup.

PER SERVING: Calories: 177; Total fat: 7g; Sodium: 156mg; Carbohydrates: 29g; Sugars: 20g; Protein: 1g

Creamed Coconut Kale

SERVES 2 TO 4
PREP TIME: 5 minutes
PRESSURE BUILD: 5 to 10 minutes

COOK TIME: 6 minutes, Sauté/High Pressure
PRESSURE RELEASE: Quick

TOTAL TIME: 16 to 21 minutes

VEGAN, UNDER 30 MINUTES

Exploding with nutrition, kale is a superstar green. It's a member of the cruciferous plant family along with illustrious veggies such as Brussels sprouts, cabbage, cauliflower, and broccoli. Kale leaves can be curly or smooth and range in color from green to purple. All colors and varieties will tenderize nicely under pressure. You can use any type of hardy leafy green in this recipe, such as collard greens, beet greens, mustard greens, and more.

1 tablespoon extra-virgin olive oil
3 garlic cloves, minced

1 bunch kale, stemmed and torn into bite-size pieces
¼ teaspoon sea salt

⅛ teaspoon freshly ground black pepper
1 cup full-fat coconut milk

1. Select Sauté on the Instant Pot. Heat the oil until it shimmers.

2. Add the garlic and sauté for 30 seconds, stirring constantly. Add the kale, salt, and pepper and stir to combine. Pour the coconut milk over the top. Press Cancel.

3. Secure the lid and seal the vent. Select Pressure Cook or Manual and cook on high pressure for 5 minutes, then quick release the pressure in the pot and remove the lid.

4. Stir the kale, and using tongs or a slotted spoon, remove to a serving bowl. Serve and enjoy!

TIP: Mix up the flavor profile by adding in a few teaspoons of minced fresh ginger.

PER SERVING: Calories: 284; Total fat: 28g; Sodium: 328mg: Carbohydrates: 9g; Sugars: 5g; Protein: 3g

Cider-Braised Brussels Sprouts

SERVES 4 TO 6
PREP TIME: 5 minutes
PRESSURE BUILD: 5 to 10 minutes

COOK TIME: 4 minutes, Sauté/High Pressure
PRESSURE RELEASE: Quick

TOTAL TIME: 14 to 19 minutes

VEGAN, NUT-FREE, UNDER 30 MINUTES

High in fiber, vitamin K, vitamin C, and many other phytonutrients, these tiny cabbages are all the rage. Brussels sprouts can be prepared in a myriad of ways, but when braised in spiced-infused apple cider, it results in sweet, veggie bliss. If you have fresh thyme, stir in 1 minced tablespoon instead of the dried at the end of step 3.

1 tablespoon extra-virgin olive oil

1 shallot, diced

1 cup apple cider or juice

1 tablespoon Dijon mustard

1 teaspoon dried thyme

½ teaspoon sea salt

¼ teaspoon freshly ground black pepper

1 pound Brussels sprouts, trimmed and halved

1. Select Sauté on the Instant Pot. Heat the oil until it shimmers.

2. Add the shallot and sauté, stirring frequently, 2 to 3 minutes, until softened and translucent. Add the apple cider, mustard, thyme, salt, and pepper. Stir to combine. Add the Brussels sprouts and stir to coat. Press Cancel.

3. Secure the lid and seal the vent. Select Pressure Cook or Manual and cook on high pressure for 1 minute, then quick release the pressure in the pot and remove the lid.

4. Using a slotted spoon, remove the Brussels sprouts to a serving bowl.

TIP: If you like crispier sprouts, try setting the cooking time to 0 minutes at high/normal pressure, then quick release the pressure in the pot.

PER SERVING: Calories: 128; Total fat: 4g; Sodium: 413mg: Carbohydrates: 21g; Sugars: 11g; Protein: 5g

"Baked" Sweet Potatoes

SERVES 4
PREP TIME: 5 minutes
PRESSURE BUILD: 5 to
10 minutes

COOK TIME: 20 to
25 minutes, High Pressure

PRESSURE RELEASE:
10 minutes, Natural
then Quick

TOTAL TIME: 40 to
50 minutes

VEGAN, NUT-FREE, UNDER
AN HOUR

Perfectly tender and creamy, these sweet potatoes are easy to make and even easier to eat. To speed things up, precut the sweet potatoes in half and reduce the cook time. Transform them into mashed sweet potatoes: after cooking, remove the skins, add a splash of coconut cream and ghee, and enjoy comfort food at its best!

4 medium sweet potatoes
Ghee (optional)

Chopped chives or scallions,
both white and green parts
(optional)
Avocado slices (optional)

Chopped, cooked bacon
(optional)

1. Place a trivet or steamer basket in the bowl of the Instant Pot and pour in 1½ cups of water.

2. Wash each sweet potato and pierce several times to create vents. Place them on the trivet, stacking as needed.

3. Secure the lid and seal the vent. Select Pressure Cook or Manual and cook for 20 minutes on high pressure, then allow the pressure to naturally release for 10 minutes. Quick release the remaining pressure in the pot and remove the lid. After cooking, if any sweet potatoes are not done enough for your liking, make sure there's at least 1 cup of water in the pot and cook for another 3 to 5 minutes, depending on how soft you want them.

4. When cool enough to handle, slice open the potatoes. If using, top with the ghee, chives, avocado slices, and bacon.

TIP: To make these in the oven, pierce each sweet potato to create vents, then bake on a baking sheet at 425°F for about 45 minutes, or until soft and easily pierced with a fork.

PER SERVING: Calories: 112; Total fat: <1g; Sodium: 72mg: Carbohydrates: 26g; Sugars: 5g; Protein: 2g

Spaghetti Squash Primavera

SERVES 2 TO 4

PREP TIME: 5 minutes

PRESSURE BUILD: 10 to 20 minutes

COOK TIME: 10 to 13 minutes, High Pressure/Sauté

PRESSURE RELEASE: Quick

TOTAL TIME: 25 to 38 minutes

VEGAN, NUT-FREE, UNDER AN HOUR

Primavera means "spring" in Italian, and this Paleo primavera showcases spring harvest veggies without the pasta. Feel free to swap in diced asparagus, zucchini, or any other spring veggie you like. To cook a plain spaghetti squash, follow steps 1 through 3 below.

1 spaghetti squash

2 tablespoons extra-virgin olive oil, divided

2 garlic cloves, minced

1 cup peas

3 tablespoons nutritional yeast

½ teaspoon sea salt

¼ teaspoon freshly ground black pepper

1 cup cherry tomatoes, halved

1. Place a trivet or steamer basket into the bowl of the Instant Pot and pour in 1½ cups of water. Cut the spaghetti squash in half crosswise and scoop out the seeds. Place both halves on the trivet, stacking if necessary.

2. Secure the lid and seal the vent. Select Pressure Cook or Manual and cook on high pressure for 7 minutes, then quick release the pressure in the pot and remove the lid. Press Cancel. If you like your squash more tender, cook under high pressure for another 1 to 3 minutes.

3. Remove the squash and set aside to cool. Empty the water from the bowl.

4. Select Sauté. Heat 1 tablespoon of oil until it shimmers. Add the garlic and cook for 30 seconds. Add the peas and cook, stirring occasionally, for 1 to 2 minutes, until softened.

5. Using a fork, scrape the squash strands from the skin and return them to the pot. Discard the skin. Stir in the nutritional yeast, salt, pepper, and remaining 1 tablespoon of oil. Gently stir in the cherry tomatoes. Serve and enjoy!

TIP: To cook a spaghetti squash whole, without cutting it, pierce a 2- to 3-pound squash all over with ½-inch cuts to create vents. Place a trivet and 1½ cups of water in the bowl and cook on high pressure for 15 to 20 minutes. Cut the squash in half and remove the seeds when cool enough to handle.

....

PER SERVING: Calories: 345; Total fat: 15g; Sodium: 678mg: Carbohydrates: 48g; Sugars: 15g; Protein: 14g

Beet Marinara Sauce

SERVES 6
PREP TIME: 10 minutes
PRESSURE BUILD: 5 to 10 minutes

COOK TIME: 13 minutes, Sauté/High Pressure
PRESSURE RELEASE: 15 minutes, Natural then Quick

TOTAL TIME: 43 to 48 minutes

VEGAN, NUT-FREE, UNDER AN HOUR

Beets are a great tomato substitute for the Autoimmune Paleo (AIP) crowd who need to avoid nightshades. Beet marinara provides a generous dose of beneficial nitric oxide, which helps regulate blood pressure and boost cognition and athletic performance. Beets also contain betalains, a powerful group of disease-fighting antioxidants.

1 tablespoon extra-virgin olive oil
1 onion, diced
2 garlic cloves, minced

6 to 8 carrots, peeled or scrubbed and chopped (about 5 cups)
2 medium beets, scrubbed and chopped (about 2 cups)
1 teaspoon sea salt, plus more as needed

¼ teaspoon freshly ground black pepper, plus more as needed
1 tablespoon dried basil
2 tablespoons freshly squeezed lemon juice

1. Select Sauté on the Instant Pot. Heat the oil until it shimmers.

2. Add the onion and garlic. Sauté for 2 to 3 minutes, stirring occasionally, until softened. Press Cancel.

3. Add the carrots, beets, salt, pepper, and 1 cup of water.

4. Secure the lid and seal the vent. Select Pressure Cook or Manual and cook on high pressure for 10 minutes, then allow the pressure to naturally release for 15 minutes. Quick release any remaining pressure in the pot and remove the lid.

5. Stir in the basil and lemon juice. Let cool for a few minutes, then puree the beet and carrot mixture—either use an immersion blender right in the pot or transfer to a standing blender. Add more water if necessary. Taste and season with more salt and pepper, if needed.

TIP: If you have fresh basil, use a small handful instead of the dried to boost the flavor.

PER SERVING: Calories: 96; Total fat: 3g; Sodium: 507mg: Carbohydrates: 18g; Sugars: 10g; Protein: 3g

Cauliflower Rice

SERVES 4

PREP TIME: 5 minutes

PRESSURE BUILD: 5 to 10 minutes

COOK TIME: 7 minutes, Sauté/High Pressure

PRESSURE RELEASE: Quick

TOTAL TIME: 17 to 22 minutes

NUT-FREE OPTION, VEGAN, UNDER 30 MINUTES

Cauliflower is the most versatile vegetable in the Paleo kingdom. It can be sautéed, roasted, boiled, mashed, or, you guessed it, riced. As rice, cauliflower adds nutrition to soups and stews, grain-free breads, waffles and pancakes, stir-fries, hashes, and more. It also makes a simple side dish, served plain or with your favorite herbs and seasonings.

1 head cauliflower, cut into small florets

½ teaspoon sea salt

¼ teaspoon freshly ground black pepper

1 tablespoon seasonings: garlic powder, ground ginger, curry powder, herbs, etc. (optional)

2 tablespoons coconut oil or ghee

1. Place the cauliflower florets into a food processor and pulse several times until they reach a grainy, rice-like consistency. Season with salt and pepper and optional seasonings (if using). Set aside.

2. Select Sauté on the Instant Pot. Heat the oil until it shimmers. Add the riced cauliflower and cook for 1 to 2 minutes, until the rice starts to soften. Press Cancel.

3. Transfer the rice to a 6- to 7-inch ceramic or heatproof bowl that fits in the Instant Pot.

4. Pour 1½ cups of water into the bowl of the Instant Pot (there's no need to wash the bits of leftover cauliflower out of it) and place a trivet at the bottom. Place the bowl of cauliflower rice on the trivet.

5. Secure the lid and seal the vent. Select Pressure Cook or Manual and cook on high pressure for 5 minutes, then quick release the pressure in the pot and remove the lid to serve.

TIP: Many supermarkets sell fresh and frozen riced cauliflower, so if you are in a hurry, pick up a bag, add seasoning, and sauté.

PER SERVING: Calories: 98; Total fat: 7g; Sodium: 336mg: Carbohydrates: 7g; Sugars: 3g; Protein: 3g

Mashed "No-tatoes"

SERVES 4
PREP TIME: 5 minutes
PRESSURE BUILD: 10 to 20 minutes

COOK TIME: 4 minutes, High Pressure
PRESSURE RELEASE: Quick

TOTAL TIME: 19 to 29 minutes

VEGETARIAN, NUT-FREE OPTION, UNDER 30 MINUTES

Although potatoes and sweet potatoes are Paleo, they are starchy carbohydrates, which you may be avoiding if you're trying to control blood sugar or lose weight. Cauliflower comes to the rescue, creating creamy, comforting, you-won't-believe-how-delicious mashed "potatoes." They taste every bit as good as the real deal with just a fraction of the calories and carbs.

1 head cauliflower, cut into large florets
2 tablespoons coconut oil or ghee

½ teaspoon sea salt
¼ teaspoon freshly ground black pepper

¼ teaspoon garlic powder
1 tablespoon chopped fresh chives (optional)

1. Place a trivet or steamer basket in the bowl of the Instant Pot and add 1½ cups of water.

2. Place the cauliflower in the Instant Pot on the trivet.

3. Secure the lid and seal the vent. Select Pressure Cook or Manual and cook for 4 minutes on high pressure, then quick release the pressure in the pot and remove the lid.

4. Remove the trivet and cauliflower and drain the water from the pot. Return just the cauliflower to the bowl.

5. Add the ghee, salt, pepper, and garlic powder. Puree in the pot using an immersion blender or mash with a masher.

6. Garnish with chives (if using) and serve.

TIP: Instead of pureeing with an immersion blender in step 5, after pressure cooking, you can transfer your cauliflower to a blender or food processor and puree with the ghee and seasonings.

PER SERVING: Calories: 94; Total fat: 7g; Sodium: 337mg: Carbohydrates: 8g; Sugars: 3g; Protein: 3g

Sesame Bok Choy

SERVES 4

PREP TIME: 5 minutes

PRESSURE BUILD: 5 to 10 minutes

COOK TIME: 1 minute, High Pressure

PRESSURE RELEASE: Quick

TOTAL TIME: 11 to 16 minutes

VEGAN, UNDER 30 MINUTES

Bok choy is an ancient Chinese veggie that belongs to the cruciferous family along with cabbage, cauliflower, and Brussels sprouts. It's a good source of beta carotene and vitamin C, as well as beneficial antioxidants and the minerals selenium, calcium, and magnesium. Cruciferous vegetables also have sulfur-containing compounds called glucosinolates that may reduce the risk of developing several chronic diseases, particularly cancer and heart disease.

1 medium head bok choy, chopped

1 tablespoon coconut aminos

1 tablespoon toasted sesame oil

2 teaspoons sesame seeds

¼ teaspoon sea salt

¼ teaspoon freshly ground black pepper

1. Place a steamer basket into the bowl of your Instant Pot and pour in 1½ cups of water.

2. Place the bok choy in the basket.

3. Secure the lid and seal the vent. Select Pressure Cook or Manual and cook on high pressure for 1 minute, then quick release the pressure in the pot and remove the lid.

4. Transfer the bok choy to a bowl and toss with the coconut aminos, oil, sesame seeds, salt, and pepper. Serve and enjoy!

TIP: Whole baby bok choy and chopped napa cabbage also work well in this recipe.

PER SERVING: Calories: 70; Total fat: 5g; Sodium: 351mg: Carbohydrates: 6g; Sugars: 3g; Protein: 4g

Gobi Masala

SERVES 4 TO 6
PREP TIME: 5 minutes
PRESSURE BUILD: 5 to 10 minutes

COOK TIME: 4 minutes, Sauté/Low Pressure
PRESSURE RELEASE: Quick

TOTAL TIME: 14 to 19 minutes

VEGETARIAN, NUT-FREE, UNDER 30 MINUTES

Gobi Masala is a vegetarian family favorite in northern India that features the popular spice garam masala. Loosely translated to "hot mix of spices," garam masala is not spicy. Rather, it's a warming spice blend, with ingredients that typically include cumin, coriander, cardamom, cloves, black pepper, cinnamon, and nutmeg. Garam masala is usually added at the end of cooking to preserve the delicate flavors and aromas.

- 1 tablespoon ghee or extra-virgin olive oil
- 1 teaspoon cumin seeds
- 1 white onion, diced
- 1 garlic clove, minced
- 1 head cauliflower, cut into florets
- 1 tablespoon ground coriander
- 1 teaspoon ground cumin
- ½ teaspoon sea salt
- ½ teaspoon garam masala

1. Select Sauté on the Instant Pot. Heat the ghee until it melts.

2. Add the cumin seeds and sauté for 30 seconds, stirring constantly. Add the onion and sauté for 1 to 2 minutes until softened. Add the garlic and sauté for 30 seconds more, stirring frequently. Press Cancel.

3. Add 1 cup of water and stir in the cauliflower, coriander, cumin, and salt.

4. Secure the lid and seal the vent. Select Pressure Cook or Manual and cook on low pressure for 1 minute, then quick release the pressure in the pot and remove the lid. Stir in the garam masala and serve.

TIP: Cumin seeds create tiny pockets of explosive flavor in this dish. If you don't have cumin seeds, you can include an additional ¾ teaspoon of ground cumin instead.

PER SERVING: Calories: 349; Total fat: 16g; Sodium: 1,358mg: Carbohydrates: 43g; Sugars: 16g; Protein: 14g

Vegetable Korma

SERVES 4 TO 6
PREP TIME: 15 minutes
PRESSURE BUILD: 10 to
20 minutes

COOK TIME: 4 minutes, High
Pressure/Low Pressure
PRESSURE RELEASE: Quick

TOTAL TIME: 29 to 39 minutes

VEGAN, UNDER AN HOUR

Traditional korma is an Indian dish featuring foods that are simmered in a small amount of yogurt, cream, or broth. This Paleo version uses coconut milk and cashew butter to yield a rich, creamy, and dairy-free vegetable korma.

1 (14-ounce) can diced
  tomatoes
1 cup full-fat coconut milk
1 small onion, chopped
2 jalapeño peppers, seeded
  and sliced
6 garlic cloves, smashed
2 teaspoons garam masala
1 teaspoon sea salt

1 teaspoon ground turmeric
½ teaspoon cumin
1 teaspoon red pepper flakes
2 tablespoons cashew butter
  or almond butter (optional)
2 small sweet potatoes,
  peeled and cut into
  1-inch chunks

2 medium carrots, cut into
  1-inch chunks
2 cups cauliflower florets
1 cup frozen green peas
½ cup chopped fresh cilantro
½ cup roasted cashews
  or almonds

1. In the bowl of the Instant Pot, combine the tomatoes with their juices and coconut milk. Add the onion, jalapeño peppers, garlic, garam masala, salt, turmeric, cumin, red pepper flakes, and cashew butter (if using). Stir to combine.

2. Place a steamer basket in the bowl on top of the sauce ingredients, then put the sweet potatoes and carrots into the basket. Secure the lid and seal the vent. Select Pressure Cook or Manual and cook on high pressure for 2 minutes, then quick release the pressure in the pot and remove the lid. Press Cancel. Remove the steamer basket and set aside.

3. Using an immersion blender, puree the sauce until smooth. Transfer the sweet potatoes and carrots into the bowl. Add the cauliflower and peas and stir to coat.

4. Secure the lid and seal the vent. Select Pressure Cook or Manual and cook on low pressure for 2 minutes, then quick release the pressure in the pot and remove the lid.

5. Garnish with the cilantro and cashews and serve.

PER SERVING: Calories: 328; Total fat: 19g; Sodium: 812mg; Carbohydrates: 35g; Sugars: 13g; Protein: 9g

Instant Pot Timing Charts

The following charts provide estimated pressure cook times for different foods when cooked at high pressure on a trivet or steamer basket with a minimum 1 cup of liquid. Times are for foods cooked alone; additional ingredients will alter the cook times.

Meat

Always use a meat thermometer to ensure beef, lamb, and pork are cooked to a minimum internal temperature of 145°F. If desired, brown/sear meats by selecting the Sauté function to seal in juices before pressure-cooking.

	MINUTES UNDER PRESSURE	RELEASE
Beef (pot roast, rump, round, chuck, blade, or brisket)	20 to 25 minutes per pound	Natural 15 minutes or more, then Quick
Beef (pot roast, rump, round, chuck, blade, or stew meat) (small chunks)	15 to 20 minutes per pound	Natural 15 minutes or more, then Quick
Beef, short ribs, bone-in	35 to 45 minutes	Natural 15 minutes or more, then Quick
Beef, sirloin steak (medium done, seared)	4 to 6 minutes	Quick
Lamb, cubes or stew meat	10 to 15 minutes per pound	Natural 15 minutes or more, then Quick
Lamb, leg, boneless	15 minutes per pound	Natural 15 minutes or more, then Quick
Pork, shoulder or butt roast	15 to 20 minutes per pound	Natural 15 minutes or more, then Quick
Pork, loin roast	15 to 20 minutes per pound	Natural 15 minutes or more, then Quick
Pork, ribs	15 to 20 minutes per pound	Natural 15 minutes or more, then Quick

Poultry

Always use a meat thermometer to ensure poultry is cooked to a minimum internal temperature of 165°F.

	MINUTES UNDER PRESSURE	RELEASE
Chicken, breasts, boneless	4 to 6 minutes	Natural 5 minutes, then Quick
Chicken, thighs, legs, or drumsticks, bone-in	22 to 30 minutes	Natural 5 minutes or more, then Quick
Chicken, wings, bone-in	10 to 25 minutes	Natural 5 to 10 minutes, then Quick
Chicken, whole	20 minutes plus 1 minute per pound	Natural 15 minutes or more
Duck, whole	25 to 45 minutes	Natural 15 minutes or more
Turkey, breast, boneless	6 to 9 minutes per pound	Natural 10 minutes or more
Turkey, drumsticks (leg)	15 to 20 minutes per pound	Natural 10 minutes or more

Fish and Seafood

Fish is done when the flesh is opaque and flakes easily with a fork. Shellfish are done when the flesh is pearly or white and opaque. Cook clams, oysters, and mussels until shells open. Discard any that do not open.

	MINUTES UNDER PRESSURE	RELEASE
Clams	2 to 4 minutes	Quick
Fish, fillet	3 to 6 minutes	Quick
Mussels	2 to 3 minutes	Quick
Shrimp or prawn	1 to 3 minutes	Quick
Crab, whole	2 to 4 minutes	Quick

Vegetables

Cooking time is for veggies cooked on a trivet and is dependent on the size of your vegetable pieces. For smaller sizes, use the shorter cooking times.

	MINUTES UNDER PRESSURE	RELEASE
Artichokes, whole	10 to 30 minutes	Quick
Beets, whole	15 to 30 minutes	Natural or Quick
Broccoli, cut into florets	2 to 4 minutes	Quick
Brussels sprouts, halved	3 to 5 minutes	Quick
Butternut squash, peeled, chopped	5 to 15 minutes	Quick
Cabbage, wedges	4 to 7 minutes	Quick
Carrots, chunks	2 to 7 minutes	Quick
Cauliflower, cut into florets	1 to 3 minutes	Quick
Green beans, whole	1 to 3 minutes	Quick
Spaghetti squash, halved lengthwise	6 to 8 minutes	Quick
Sweet potatoes, whole	15 to 25 minutes	Natural 10 minutes, then Quick

Measurement Conversions

VOLUME EQUIVALENTS	US STANDARD	US STANDARD (OUNCES)	METRIC (APPROXIMATE)
LIQUID	2 tablespoons	1 fl. oz.	30 mL
	¼ cup	2 fl. oz.	60 mL
	½ cup	4 fl. oz.	120 mL
	1 cup	8 fl. oz.	240 mL
	1½ cups	12 fl. oz.	355 mL
	2 cups or 1 pint	16 fl. oz.	475 mL
	4 cups or 1 quart	32 fl. oz.	1 L
	1 gallon	128 fl. oz.	4 L
DRY	⅛ teaspoon	–	0.5 mL
	¼ teaspoon	–	1 mL
	½ teaspoon	–	2 mL
	¾ teaspoon	–	4 mL
	1 teaspoon	–	5 mL
	1 tablespoon	–	15 mL
	¼ cup	–	59 mL
	⅓ cup	–	79 mL
	½ cup	–	118 mL
	⅔ cup	–	156 mL
	¾ cup	–	177 mL
	1 cup	–	235 mL
	2 cups or 1 pint	–	475 mL
	3 cups	–	700 mL
	4 cups or 1 quart	–	1 L
	½ gallon	–	2 L
	1 gallon	–	4 L

OVEN TEMPERATURES

FAHRENHEIT	CELSIUS (APPROXIMATE)
250°F	120°C
300°F	150°C
325°F	165°C
350°F	180°C
375°F	190°C
400°F	200°C
425°F	220°C
450°F	230°C

WEIGHT EQUIVALENTS

US STANDARD	METRIC (APPROXIMATE)
½ ounce	15 g
1 ounce	30 g
2 ounces	60 g
4 ounces	115 g
8 ounces	225 g
12 ounces	340 g
16 ounces or 1 pound	455 g

Resources

The following resources provide a wealth of science-backed, cutting-edge health information from the world's leading Paleo authorities.

The Paleo 30-Day Challenge cookbook by Kinsey Jackson and Sally Johnson is packed with 75 delicious recipes, four weeks of meal plans, and plenty of beginner-friendly information.

PaleoHacks.com covers everything Paleo with resources, books, and recipes to make living a Paleo lifestyle easy.

PaleoPlan.com offers customizable Paleo meal plans, hundreds of free recipes, and at-home bodyweight workouts designed by a team of health experts.

RobbWolf.com provides science-based information about the Paleo and Keto diets. Best-selling author Robb Wolf also leads and hosts The Healthy Rebellion and its podcast.

ChrisKresser.com offers evidence-based information and training. Chris Kresser is a leading authority in the fields of Functional Medicine and the Paleo diet.

MarksDailyApple.com is the website of Mark Sisson, who shares research-based information and actionable tips for living Primal and Keto lifestyles.

nomnompaleo.com is the website of Michelle Tam, who shares hundreds of award-winning Paleo recipes, cookbooks, meal plans, and more.

ThePaleoDiet.com provides books, research, and recipes by Dr. Loren Cordain, the man considered to be the modern-day founder of the Paleo diet.

ThePaleoMom.com is the website of Dr. Sarah Ballantyne, the foremost authority on the Autoimmune Protocol (AIP) of the Paleo Diet.

Whole30.com is the hub for the Whole30 challenge, founded by Melissa Urban.

References

Astrup, Arne, Faidon Magkos, Dennis M. Bier, et al. "Saturated Fats and Health:
  A Reassessment and Proposal for Food-Based Recommendations: JACC
  State-of-the-Art Review." *Journal of the American College of Cardiology* 76, no. 7
  (August 2020): 844–57. doi: 10.1016/j.jacc.2020.05.077.

Barone, Monica, Silvia Turroni, Simone Rampelli, et al. "Gut Microbiome Response
  to a Modern Paleolithic Diet in a Western Lifestyle Context." *PLoS ONE* 14, no. 8
  (August 2019): e0220619. doi: 10.1371/journal.pone.0220619.

Bazzano, Lydia A, Tian Hu, Kristi Reynolds, et al. "Effects of Low-Carbohydrate and
  Low-Fat Diets: A Randomized Trial." *Annals of Internal Medicine* 161, no. 5
  (September 2014): 309–18. doi: 10.7326/M14-0180.

Cordain, Loren, S. Boyd Eaton, Anthony Sebastian, et al. "Origins and Evolution of the
  Western Diet: Health Implications for the 21st Century." *The American Journal of
  Clinical Nutrition* 81, no. 2 (February 2005): 341–54. doi: 10.1093/ajcn.81.2.341.

Cordain, Loren, and Joe Friel. *The Paleo Diet for Athletes: The Ancient Nutritional
  Formula for Peak Athletic Performance.* New York: Rodale, 2012.

Dehghan, Mahshid, Andrew Mente, Xiaohe Zhang, et al. "Associations of Fats and
  Carbohydrate Intake with Cardiovascular Disease and Mortality in 18 Countries
  from Five Continents (PURE): A Prospective Cohort Study." *Lancet* 390, no. 10107
  (November 2017): 2050–2062. doi: 10.1016/S0140-6736(17)32252-3.

Deol, Jasraj, K., and Kiran Bains. "Effect of Household Cooking Methods on Nutritional and Anti Nutritional Factors in Green Cowpea (*Vigna unguiculata*) Pods."
  Journal of Food Science and Technology 47, no. 5 (October 2010): 579–81.
  doi: 10.1007/s13197-010-0112-3.

De Punder, Karin, and Leo Pruimboom. "The Dietary Intake of Wheat and Other
  Cereal Grains and Their Role in Inflammation." *Nutrients* 5, no. 3 (March 2013):
  771-87. doi: 10.3390/nu5030771.

Fasano, Alessio. "Zonulin and Its Regulation of Intestinal Barrier Function: The
  Biological Door to Inflammation, Autoimmunity, and Cancer." *Physiological
  Reviews* 91, no. 1 (January 2011): 151–75. doi: 10.1152/physrev.00003.2008.

Frassetto, L. A., M. Schloetter, M. Mietus-Synder, et al. "Metabolic and Physiologic
  Improvements from Consuming a Paleolithic, Hunter-Gatherer Type Diet."
  European Journal of Clinical Nutrition 63, no. 8 (August 2009): 947–55.
  doi: 10.1038/ejcn.2009.4.

Galgano, F., F. Favati, M. Caruso, et al. "The Influence of Processing and Preservation on the Retention of Health-Promoting Compounds in Broccoli." *Journal of Food Science* 72, no. 2 (March 2007): S130–35. doi: 10.1111/j.1750-3841.2006.00258.x.

Ghaedi, Ehsan, Mohammad Mohammadi, Hamed Mohammadi, et al. "Effects of a Paleolithic Diet on Cardiovascular Disease Risk Factors: A Systematic Review and Meta-Analysis of Randomized Controlled Trials." *Advances in Nutrition* 10, no. 4 (July 2019): 634–46. doi: 10.1093/advances/nmz007.

Jönsson, Tommy, Yvonne Granfeldt, Bo Ahrén, et al. "Beneficial Effects of a Paleolithic Diet on Cardiovascular Risk Factors in Type 2 Diabetes: A Randomized Cross-Over Pilot Study." *Cardiovascular Diabetology* 8, no. 35 (July 2009). doi: 10.1186/1475-2840-8-35.

Lindeberg S., T. Jönsson, Y. Granfeldt, et al. "A Palaeolithic Diet Improves Glucose Tolerance More Than a Mediterranean-Like Diet in Individuals with Ischaemic Heart Disease." *Diabetologia* 50, no. 9 (September 2007): 1795–1807. doi: 10.1007/s00125-007-0716-y.

Manheimer, Eric W., Esther J. van Zuuren, Zbys Fedorowicz, et al. "Paleolithic Nutrition for Metabolic Syndrome: Systematic Review and Meta-Analysis." *American Journal of Clinical Nutrition* 102, no. 4 (October 2015): 922–32. doi: 10.3945/ajcn.115.113613.

Martin, C. A., and J. Akers. "Paleo Diet versus Modified Paleo Diet: A Randomized Control Trial of Weight Loss and Biochemical Benefit." *Journal of the Academy of Nutrition and Dietetics* 113, no. 9 (September 2013): A35. doi: 10.1016/j.jand.2013.06.115.

Otten J., A. Stomby, M. Waling, A. Isaksson, et al. "A Heterogeneous Response of Liver and Skeletal Muscle Fat to the Combination of a Paleolithic Diet and Exercise in Obese Individuals with Type 2 Diabetes: A Randomised Controlled Trial." *Diabetologia* 61, no. 7 (July 2018): 1548–59. doi: 10.1007/s00125-018-4618-y.

Pastore, R. L., Judith T. Brooks, and John W. Carbone. "Paleolithic Nutrition Improves Plasma Lipid Concentrations of Hypercholesterolemic Adults to a Greater Extent Than Traditional Heart-Healthy Dietary Recommendations." *Nutrition Research* 35, no. 6 (June 2015): 474–79. doi: 10.1016/j.nutres.2015.05.002.

Ryberg, M., S. Sandberg, C. Mellberg, et al. "A Palaeolithic-Type diet Causes Strong Tissue-Specific Effects on Ectopic Fat Deposition in Obese Postmenopausal Women." *Journal of Internal Medicine* 274, no. 1 (July 2013): 67–76. doi: 10.1111/joim.12048.

Sturgeon, Craig, and Alessio Fasano. "Zonulin, a Regulator of Epithelial and Endothelial Barrier Functions, and Its Involvement in Chronic Inflammatory Diseases." *Tissue Barriers* 4, no. 4 (October 2016): e1251384. doi: 10.1080/21688370.2016.1251384.

Whalen K. A., M. L. McCullough, W. D. Flanders, et al. "Paleolithic and Mediterranean Diet Pattern Scores Are Inversely Associated with Biomarkers of Inflammation and Oxidative Balance in Adults." *The Journal of Nutrition* 146, no. 6 (June 2016): 1217–26. doi: 10.3945/jn.115.224048.

Xu, Baojun, and Sam K. C. Chang. "Effect of Soaking, Boiling, and Steaming on Total Phenolic Content and Antioxidant Activities of Cool Season Food Legumes." *Food Chemistry* 110, no. 1 (September 2008): 1–13. doi: 10.1016/j.foodchem.2008.01.045.

Yadav, S. K., and S. Sehgal. "Effect of Home Processing on Ascorbic Acid and Beta-Carotene Content of Spinach (*Spinacia oleracia*) and Amaranth (*Amaranthus tricolor*) Leaves." *Plant Foods for Human Nutrition* 47, no. 2 (February 1995): 125–31. doi: 10.1007/BF01089261.

Index

A

Almond Cod, 69
Altitude adjustments, 22
Anti-block shield, 18
Apples
  Grain-Free Bircher Bowls with Yogurt, 35
  Pork Roast with Apples, 95
  Sweet Potato Breakfast Bowls, 34
Artichokes
  Lemon-Steamed Artichokes, 104
  pressure cooker cook times, 121
Asparagus, Herbed, 105
Avocados
  Chicken Taco Soup, 43
  Green Veggie Frittata, 29

B

Baby Back Instant Pot Ribs, 100
Bacon and Eggs, "Cheesy," 32
"Baked" Sweet Potatoes, 109
Barbacoa Beef, 79
Beans, 5, 121
Beef
  Barbacoa Beef, 79
  Beef and Broccoli, 85
  Beef Goulash, 38
  Beef Stroganoff, 88
  Corned Beef and Cabbage, 86
  Hearty Beef Chili, 82
  Instant Meatballs, 80
  Korean-Inspired Short Ribs, 89
  Moroccan-Inspired Beef, 83
  Pizza Soup, 47
  Pot Roast with Winter Vegetables, 87
  pressure cooker cook times, 119
  Roast Beef and Roots, 78
  Sweet and Sour Meatloaf, 81
  Thai-Inspired Red Curry Beef, 84

Beets
  Beet Marinara Sauce, 111
  pressure cooker cook times, 121
Bircher Bowls, Grain-Free, with Yogurt, 35
Blackberry-Glazed Pork Chops, 96
Blueberry-Coconut Chia Porridge, 33
Bok Choy, Sesame, 114
Bone Broth in an Instant, 40
Breakfast Bowls, Sweet Potato, 34
Broccoli
  Beef and Broccoli, 85
  Cilantro-Coconut Shrimp and Broccoli, 72
  pressure cooker cook times, 121
Broth, Bone, in an Instant, 40
Brussels sprouts
  Cider-Braised Brussels Sprouts, 108
  pressure cooker cook times, 121
Buffalo Chicken Wings, 57
BURN message, 19

C

Cabbage
  Corned Beef and Cabbage, 86
  pressure cooker cook times, 121
Calcium, 9
Carnitas, Pork, 92
Carrots
  Beet Marinara Sauce, 111
  Corned Beef and Cabbage, 86
  Pot Roast with Winter Vegetables, 87
  pressure cooker cook times, 121
  Roast Beef and Roots, 78
  Spanish-Inspired Pork, 93
  Vegetable Korma, 116
  Whole "Roasted" Chicken with Vegetables, 53

Cashews
    Cashew Chicken, 58–59
    Vegetable Korma, 116
Cauliflower
    Cauliflower Rice, 112
    Chicken "Pozole" Verde, 44
    Gobi Masala, 115
    Mac 'n' Cheese 'n' Ham, 97
    Mashed "No-tatoes," 113
    pressure cooker cook times, 121
    Sausage-Stuffed Peppers, 101
    Vegetable Korma, 116
"Cheesy" Bacon and Eggs, 32
Chia seeds
    Coconut-Blueberry Chia Porridge, 33
    Grain-Free Bircher Bowls with Yogurt, 35
Chicken
    Buffalo Chicken Wings, 57
    Cashew Chicken, 58–59
    Chicken Cacciatore, 52
    Chicken "Pozole" Verde, 44
    Chicken Taco Soup, 43
    Easy Chicken Fajitas, 51
    Herbed Chicken with Olives, 54
    Instant Meatballs, 80
    Lemon Chicken, 55
    Perfect Chicken Breast, 50
    pressure cooker cook times, 120
    30-Minute Chile Chicken, 56
    Whole "Roasted" Chicken
       with Vegetables, 53
Chiles
    Barbacoa Beef, 79
    Chicken "Pozole" Verde, 44
    Pork Green Chili, 46
    30-Minute Chile Chicken, 56
Chili
    Game-Day Chili, 60
    Hearty Beef Chili, 82
    Pork Green Chili, 46
Cider-Braised Brussels Sprouts, 108
Cilantro
    Chicken "Pozole" Verde, 44
    Cilantro-Coconut Shrimp and Broccoli, 72
    Pork Green Chili, 46

Clams
    Clams Steamed in Lemon-Garlic Broth, 74
    pressure cooker cook times, 120
Coconut
    Cilantro-Coconut Shrimp and Broccoli, 72
    Coconut-Blueberry Chia Porridge, 33
    Coconut Fish Curry, 68
    Creamed Coconut Kale, 107
Cod, Almond, 69
Condensation collector, 18
Corned Beef and Cabbage, 86
Crab, pressure cooker cook times, 120
Creamed Coconut Kale, 107
Creamy Butternut Soup, 39
Curried dishes
    Coconut Fish Curry, 68
    Thai-Inspired Red Curry Beef, 84

D

Dairy, 6
Day-After-Thanksgiving Soup, 45
Delay Start or Timer button, 21
Dill Sauce, Poached Salmon with, 70
Duck
    Duck with Mushrooms and
       Pearl Onions, 62
    pressure cooker cook times, 120

E

Easy Chicken Fajitas, 51
Easy Hawaiian-Style Pork, 94
Eggplant
    Eggs in Purgatory, 30
Eggs
    "Cheesy" Bacon and Eggs, 32
    Eggs in Purgatory, 30
    Green Veggie Frittata, 29
    Hard- and Soft-Boiled Eggs, 28
Equipment, 11

F

Fajitas, Chicken, Easy, 51
Fats, 4–5
Fennel and Leeks, Pumpkin Soup with, 41
15-Minute Mediterranean Halibut, 67

Fish
    Almond Cod, 69
    Coconut Fish Curry, 68
    15-Minute Mediterranean Halibut, 67
    Poached Salmon with Dill Sauce, 70
    pressure cooker cook times, 120
    Salmon and Vegetables en Papillote, 71
    Seafood Gumbo, 73
    Steamed Fish and Veggies, 66
Float valve, 17
Food allergies, 8
Frittata, Green Veggie, 29
Fruits, 5. *See also specific fruits*

G

Game-Day Chili, 60
Garlic-Lemon Broth, Clams
        Steamed in, 74
Gobi Masala, 115
Goulash, Beef, 38
Grain-Free Bircher Bowls with
        Yogurt, 35
Grains, 5
Green Veggie Frittata, 29
Gumbo, Seafood, 73

H

Halibut
    15-Minute Mediterranean
        Halibut, 67
    Seafood Gumbo, 73
Ham
    Holiday Honey Ham, 99
    Mac 'n' Cheese 'n' Ham, 97
Hard- and Soft-Boiled Eggs, 28
Hash, Spicy Sausage and "No-tato," 31
Hearty Beef Chili, 82
Herbs. *See also specific herbs*
    Almond Cod, 69
    Herbed Asparagus, 105
    Herbed Chicken with Olives, 54
Holiday Honey Ham, 99
Honey
    Holiday Honey Ham, 99
    Honey Mustard Pork Tenderloin, 98

I

Inner pot, 18
Instant Meatballs, 80
Instant Pot
    3-quart Mini, about, 16
    altitude adjustments, 22
    benefits of, 12, 16
    cleaning, 24
    cooking Paleo recipes in, 23–24
    functions, 19–22
    models of, 16
    parts of the, 17–19
    pressure cook time charts, 119–121
    safety precautions, 23

K

Kale
    "Cheesy" Bacon and Eggs, 32
    Creamed Coconut Kale, 107
Keep Warm/Cancel function, 21
Keto diet, 9
Kitchen tools, 11
Korean-Inspired Short Ribs, 89
Korma, Vegetable, 116

L

Lamb
    Instant Meatballs, 80
    pressure cooker cook times, 119
LCD display, 20
Leeks and Fennel, Pumpkin
        Soup with, 41
Legumes, 5
Lemon
    Clams Steamed in Lemon-Garlic
        Broth, 74
    Lemon Chicken, 55
    Lemon-Steamed Artichokes, 104
Lid, 17

M

Mac 'n' Cheese 'n' Ham, 97
Maple-Balsamic Parsnips, 106
Marinara Sauce, Beet, 111

Mashed "No-tatoes," 113

Measuring cup, 19

Meat. *See also* Beef; Lamb; Pork

    pressure cooker cook times, 119

Meatballs, Instant, 80

Meatloaf, Sweet and Sour, 81

Moroccan-Inspired Beef, 83

Mushrooms

    Duck with Mushrooms and

        Pearl Onions, 62

    Pizza Soup, 47

    Salmon and Vegetables en Papillote, 71

Mussels

    pressure cooker cook times, 120

    Steamed Mussels with White

        Wine Sauce, 75

N

Natural release, 22

Nutritional yeast

    "Cheesy" Bacon and Eggs, 32

    Mac 'n' Cheese 'n' Ham, 97

    Spaghetti Squash Primavera, 110

Nuts

    Almond Cod, 69

    Cashew Chicken, 58–59

    Coconut-Blueberry Chia

        Porridge, 33

    Vegetable Korma, 116

O

Olives

    15-Minute Mediterranean Halibut, 67

    Hearty Beef Chili, 82

    Herbed Chicken with Olives, 54

    Moroccan-Inspired Beef, 83

Onions, Pearl, and Mushrooms,

    Duck with, 62

Outer pot, 18

P

Paleo diet

    body's adaptation to, 8

    defined, 2

    health benefits, 3

    ingredient staples for, 10

    nutritional breakdown, 3–7

    Q&As, 8–9

    removing non-Paleo foods, 11

    science behind, 2

    where and what to buy, 8

Parsnips

    Maple-Balsamic Parsnips, 106

    Pot Roast with Winter Vegetables, 87

    Spanish-Inspired Pork, 93

Peas

    Salmon and Vegetables en

        Papillote, 71

    Spaghetti Squash Primavera, 110

    Steamed Fish and Veggies, 66

    Vegetable Korma, 116

Peppers. *See also* Chiles

    Beef Goulash, 38

    Chicken Cacciatore, 52

    Easy Chicken Fajitas, 51

    Sausage-Stuffed Peppers, 101

    Thai-Inspired Red Curry Beef, 84

Perfect Chicken Breast, 50

Pineapple

    Easy Hawaiian-Style Pork, 94

Pizza Soup, 47

Plastic rice paddle, 19

Poached Salmon with Dill Sauce, 70

Pork. *See also* Ham; Sausages

    Baby Back Instant Pot Ribs, 100

    Blackberry-Glazed Pork Chops, 96

    "Cheesy" Bacon and Eggs, 32

    Easy Hawaiian-Style Pork, 94

    Honey Mustard Pork Tenderloin, 98

    Pork Carnitas, 92

    Pork Green Chili, 46

    Pork Roast with Apples, 95

    pressure cooker cook times, 119

    Sausage-Stuffed Peppers, 101

    Spanish-Inspired Pork, 93

Porridge, Coconut-Blueberry Chia, 33

Pot Roast with Winter Vegetables, 87

Poultry. *See also* Chicken; Duck; Turkey

    pressure cooker cook times, 120

Pressure, releasing, 22

Pressure Cook/Manual button, 20
Protein, 4
Pumpkin Soup with Fennel and Leeks, 41

Q

Quick cook settings, 20–21
Quick release, 22

R

Restaurant meals, 9
Rice paddle, 19
Ring, 17
Roast Beef and Roots, 78

S

Salmon
  Poached Salmon with Dill Sauce, 70
  Salmon and Vegetables en
    Papillote, 71
Salt, 6
Sauce, Beet Marinara, 111
Sausages
  Pizza Soup, 47
  Sausage-Stuffed Peppers, 101
  Spicy Sausage and "No-tato" Hash, 31
Sauté function, 21
Seafood. See also Fish; Shellfish
  Seafood Gumbo, 73
Seeds. See also Chia seeds
  Grain-Free Bircher Bowls with Yogurt, 35
  Sesame Bok Choy, 114
Sesame Bok Choy, 114
Shellfish
  Cilantro-Coconut Shrimp and Broccoli, 72
  Clams Steamed in Lemon-Garlic Broth, 74
  pressure cooker cook times, 120
  Seafood Gumbo, 73
  Steamed Mussels with White
    Wine Sauce, 75
Shrimp
  Cilantro-Coconut Shrimp and
    Broccoli, 72
  pressure cooker cook times, 120
  Seafood Gumbo, 73
Silicone sealing ring, 17

Slow Cook button, 21
Soups
  Chicken Taco Soup, 43
  Creamy Butternut Soup, 39
  Day-After-Thanksgiving Soup, 45
  Pizza Soup, 47
  Pumpkin Soup with Fennel and Leeks, 41
Soup spoon, 19
Spaghetti Squash Primavera, 110
Spanish-Inspired Pork, 93
Spices, 6
Spicy Sausage and "No-tato" Hash, 31
Spinach
  Green Veggie Frittata, 29
  Sweet Potato and "Pea-not" Stew, 42
Squash. See also Zucchini
  Creamy Butternut Soup, 39
  pressure cooker cook times, 121
  Pumpkin Soup with Fennel and Leeks, 41
  Spaghetti Squash Primavera, 110
Steamed Fish and Veggies, 66
Steamed Mussels with White
    Wine Sauce, 75
Steamer rack, 18
Steam release valve, 17
Stews
  Chicken "Pozole" Verde, 44
  Moroccan-Inspired Beef, 83
  Sweet Potato and "Pea-not" Stew, 42
Stroganoff, Beef, 88
Sugars, 6
Supplements, 9
Sweet and Sour Meatloaf, 81
Sweet potatoes
  "Baked" Sweet Potatoes, 109
  Beef Goulash, 38
  Day-After-Thanksgiving Soup, 45
  Game-Day Chili, 60
  Hearty Beef Chili, 82
  pressure cooker cook times, 121
  Roast Beef and Roots, 78
  Spicy Sausage and "No-tato" Hash, 31
  Sweet Potato and "Pea-not" Stew, 42
  Sweet Potato Breakfast Bowls, 34
Vegetable Korma, 116

T

Thai-Inspired Red Curry Beef, 84
30-Minute Chile Chicken, 56
Tomatillos
  Chicken "Pozole" Verde, 44
  Pork Green Chili, 46
Tomatoes
  Beef Goulash, 38
  Chicken Cacciatore, 52
  Eggs in Purgatory, 30
  15-Minute Mediterranean Halibut, 67
  Game-Day Chili, 60
  Hearty Beef Chili, 82
  Instant Meatballs, 80
  Pizza Soup, 47
  Salmon and Vegetables en Papillote, 71
  Seafood Gumbo, 73
  Spaghetti Squash Primavera, 110
  Steamed Fish and Veggies, 66
  Thai-Inspired Red Curry Beef, 84
  30-Minute Chile Chicken, 56
  Turkey Bolognese, 61
  Vegetable Korma, 116
Turkey
  Day-After-Thanksgiving Soup, 45
  Game-Day Chili, 60
  Instant Meatballs, 80
  pressure cooker cook times, 120
  Turkey Bolognese, 61

V

Vegetables, 5. *See also specific vegetables*
Pot Roast with Winter Vegetables, 87
pressure cooker cook times, 121
Vegetable Korma, 116

W

Wheat, 5
Whole30, 9
Whole "Roasted" Chicken with Vegetables, 53

Y

Yogurt, Grain-Free Bircher Bowls with, 35

Z

Zucchini
  Day-After-Thanksgiving Soup, 45
  Pork Green Chili, 46
  Steamed Fish and Veggies, 66
  Thai-Inspired Red Curry Beef, 84

Acknowledgments

Kinsey Jackson

Good health starts in the home and is rooted in the love of family. I am so lucky to have married the most loving, caring, and brilliant man I have ever known. Thank you, Matt, for your unending support and for teaching me that love speaks louder than words. To my darling Milagro, you are a daily reminder that miracles come to life when we dare to dream. To my mother, Alicia, you light up my life; your humor and compassion are medicine, and I cherish our friendship more each passing day. And to my soul sister Sally: Just when I thought Paleo couldn't get any better, you came along . . . the bacon to my eggs . . . and filled my pen with the ink of inspiration. Thank you, family—your love and support are the very foundation that this book was built upon.

Sally Johnson

The road to health is a personal journey, but it isn't traveled alone. On my Paleo journey that led to the writing of this book, I was inspired, motivated, and supported by my loving family and so many of my friends. A very special thanks goes out to my co-author, Kinsey, not only for being the best writing partner I could ever hope for but for being a great friend as well. To my loving mother, thank you for always inspiring me beyond words and initiating me into the world of nutrition. To my CrossFit community, thank you for lighting the spark and always pushing me to be the best version of myself. To my husband and children, thank you for eating my Paleo meals. They are always prepared with love.

About the Authors

Kinsey Jackson

Kinsey Jackson, MS, CNS, CFMP, is a certified nutrition specialist clinician and certified functional medicine practitioner with a master of science in human nutrition. She specializes in the connection between diet and disease and has worked in the healthcare field for over two decades. After following a vegetarian diet for nearly 25 years, she was diagnosed with multiple crippling autoimmune diseases. By adopting a Paleo lifestyle, she was able to eat her way back to health using food as her medicine. This experience vastly contributes to her passion for helping others reclaim their vitality by making informed dietary decisions. She has over a decade of experience leading Paleo challenges and has worked with thousands of people worldwide. You can learn more about Kinsey at her website, KinseyJackson.com.

Sally Johnson

Sally Johnson, MA, RD, LD, CFMP is a registered and licensed dietitian in Texas with a master's in applied physiology. She specializes in ancestrally based nutrition and lifestyle practices and is a certified functional medicine practitioner and primal health coach. Sally reversed her own health issues with functional nutrition and CrossFit and now coaches clients on how to optimize their health and improve their body composition and physiology. You can learn more at her website, SallyJohnsonRD.com.

CPSIA information can be obtained
at www.ICGtesting.com
Printed in the USA
JSHW041904121121
20395JS00004B/36